Political Behavior
of the
American Electorate

Political Behavior
of the
American Electorate

William H. Flanigan
University of Minnesota

ALLYN AND BACON, INC.
BOSTON

Library of Congress Card Catalog Number: 68–15406

PRINTED IN THE UNITED STATES OF AMERICA

FIRST PRINTING . . . JANUARY, 1968
SECOND PRINTING . . . SEPTEMBER, 1968

To My Parents

———◆———

Acknowledgments

THE FOLLOWING ANALYSIS AND DESCRIPTION OF THE AMERICAN ELEC-torate is heavily dependent on the work of others. Until recently, extensive analysis of the research findings and data collected by another social scientist was limited to an examination of published tables, but there have been significant changes since 1960. The major studies of American public opinion and voting behavior are now available to scholars throughout the world for further analysis and examination.

These developments in political analysis have depended on the cooperation of many individuals, but the efforts of two men associated with the Survey Research Center at the University of Michigan deserve special mention. For a number of years Angus Campbell has opened the archives of the Survey Research Center to outside scholars, and I have drawn on the work of many, most notably V. O. Key, who have benefited from the generosity and assistance of Angus Campbell and the Survey Research Center. Warren Miller has directed the organization and expansion of these activities through the creation of the Inter-university Consortium for Political Research. The Consortium which is composed of the Survey Research Center and about one hundred departments of political science has not only made available the archives of the Survey Research Center to a much wider clientele but has made available other major data collections on the same basis.

This study is completely dependent on Survey Research Center data provided by the Inter-university Consortium for Political Research, and I am pleased to acknowledge my great debt to the individuals in both organizations who have contributed to the establishment of these resources and services. I must hasten to add that neither the Survey Research Center nor the Consortium bears any responsibility for the analyses and interpretations presented here. Indeed the hazard of their efforts to provide open archives is the sort of reinterpretation and reanalysis which follows, and I can only hope that the weaknesses of this work will not reflect on the general worthiness and excellence of the Corsortium and the Survey Research Center.

I must also express my debt to the director of the Social Science Research Facilities Center at the University of Minnesota for his assistance with the data processing and to Gloria Priem for typing the manuscript. Among the many students at Minnesota who helped with the analysis I am particularly indebted to Doug Frisbie, Caroline Harlow, John Pierce, and Nancy Zingale for genially and competently handling so many of the laborious details in the preparation of the tables. Again these acknowledgments do not diminish my responsibility for the errors that follow, but they qualify considerably the credit I am due.

W. H. F.

Contents

List of Illustrations
and Tables

Political Behavior
of the
American Electorate

Introduction

————◆————

THE AMERICAN ELECTORAL SYSTEM IS ONE OF THE MOST FASCINATING of all political institutions. Not only do American campaigns and elections provide a colorful and entertaining array of political practices, but in the United States the political party system, the candidates' appeal to the public, and the ultimate selection and rejection of political leaders represent a successful and time-tested democratic decision-making mechanism the equal of any in human history. For all that, the American electoral system does not operate perfectly and in some ways it does not operate well at all. This introductory text is not an evaluation of the American electoral system; rather, it will explore the system's behavior during the past couple of decades. Voting behavior and political opinions of the American public as well as some explanations of these major political patterns are the central concerns of this volume.

The public appears as a concept in discussions of democratic politics and in a general sense the meaning of the term is clear. However, there are a number of different specific ways to define the public in the United States as an analytic focus for the study of political behavior. There are several choices for the meaning of the public: the citizenry, the voters and those who influence policy. First, and perhaps most obvious, is a definition of the public as all individuals in the society who have the right to vote, the citizenry. There are good reasons for using suffrage or the right to vote as a basis for determining who is in the public and who is not. The right to vote is a fundamental element of political power. Democratic political theory argues that the enfranchised are more influential, more adequately represented than the disfranchised. Presumably the public to which democratic political leaders respond is the political electorate, and if our goal is increased understanding of the role of the public in policy formation and the operation of our government, suffrage is the proper basis for defining the public.

There are several reasons for not being content with suffrage alone to define the public. For one thing, under some circumstances individuals who do not have the right to vote may become important in influencing policy and political leaders. Women, for example, were a significant political force before they had suffrage. They not only exerted influence to acquire the vote but joined in a variety of reform movements. More significantly, under many circumstances large numbers of eligible voters neither vote nor involve themselves in any way in the political decision-making of the community. To better examine the impact of the mass of individuals on the leaders' policy-making, one might define the public simply as all the individuals whose activities or attitudes influence policy in any way. This is a straightforward description of the public for most analytic purposes, but it would be most impractical to determine in a complex society which individuals have any influence on any of the policies of the society. This definition of the public might be used with greater hope of success in studying a single policy decision, but the simplicity of a single decision might be deceptive since, under careful scrutiny, decisions that have appeared independent of one another are found to be interrelated. There is an additional complication: individuals may influence decisions without at first appearing to and without intending to. If decision-makers take individuals into account when making policy, then those individuals have some influence over policy and by our definition are to be included in the public. Having influence by being taken into account can cover individuals who could not exert influence any other way. In a slave society where slaves are "powerless" they may be taken into account by leaders who moderate certain policies or refrain from others for fear the slaves will revolt. The slaves would still not be powerful but they would have some influence and consequently be part of the public.

A third possibility for a definition of the public is the individuals in a society who actually vote. This is something of a compromise between all those eligible to vote and those with some influence over policies. It is relatively easy to identify the voters, say, in contrast to individuals with influence, and the argument for using voters as our definition would be that voting is an act of influence.

The many studies employed in the course of this book have used a wide range of definitions of public and a single definition will not be selected and used consistently throughout. Rather, aspects of political behavior which entail different definitions of the public will be investigated. No great care will be given to moving from one implicit definition to another, although greater attention to this analytic category is a plausible and desirable next step in political analysis.

MAJOR VOTING STUDIES

It is easy to categorize the major voting studies of the American electorate according to the scholars and research institutions that conducted the studies. The first study of voting behavior and political opinion relying on survey research techniques was directed by Paul Lazarsfeld, who was interested in the impact of mass media on individual vote choice during a Presidential campaign. Lazarsfeld selected a single community, Erie County in Ohio, for his study during the 1940 Presidential campaign, and when he published the findings, *The People's Choice*,[1] it became a major work of social analysis. In 1948 Lazarsfeld, Bernard Berelson, and William McPhee of the Bureau of Applied Social Research at Columbia University conducted a second political study in Elmira, New York, and published their findings in *Voting*.[2] Several major findings in political research emerged from these two studies: the cross pressure hypothesis, opinion leadership, selective perception. To this point the important studies were of single communities and conducted entirely by sociologists.

In 1948 the newspaper polls predicted a Republican victory in the Dewey-Truman race for President while a Survey Research Center national survey showed Truman winning, thereby publicizing the more scientific sampling used in academic polling. This success promoted a national political survey during the 1952 Presidential election, which was reported in *The Voter Decides*[3] and which emphasized partisanship, issues, and candidate images. National political studies have been made by the Survey Research Center every two years since 1952 and the following analysis depends heavily on these studies up to and including the 1964 survey. The most impressive study, *The American Voter*[4] by Campbell, Converse, Miller and Stokes, was based mainly on the 1952 and 1956 national surveys and continued the

---

[1] Paul Lazarsfeld, Bernard Berelson and Hazel Gaudet, *The People's Choice* (New York: Columbia University Press, 1944).

[2] Bernard R. Berelson, Paul F. Lazarsfeld and William N. McPhee, *Voting* (Chicago: University of Chicago Press, 1954).

[3] Angus Campbell, Gerald Gurin and Warren Miller, *The Voter Decides* (Evanston: Row, Peterson and Co., 1954).

[4] Angus Campbell *et al.*, *The American Voter* (New York: John Wiley and Sons, 1960).

emphasis on partisanship and political attitudes. It is required reading for anyone with a serious interest in American political behavior. Most of the following analysis depends heavily on *The American Voter*, both for substantive findings about the electorate and for analytic organization of the material. The most recent publication by these authors, *Elections and the Political Order*,[5] covers subsequent elections and pursues the main themes of *The American Voter* in more complex analysis.

The most extensive survey of research on American political behavior is *Political Life*[6] by Robert Lane and this might be supplemented by bibliographic essays in *Essays on the Behavioral Study of Politics*[7] edited by Austin Ranney or *The Behavioral Persuasion in Politics*[8] by Heinz Eulau. The best collections of readings on political behavior currently available appear to be *Political Opinion and Electoral Behavior*[9] by Dreyer and Rosenbaum and *Politics and Social Life*[10] by Polsby, Dentler and Smith. Several recent studies of importance deal with special topics. A highly sophisticated analysis of Negro political behavior in the South is *Negroes and the New Southern Politics*[11] by Matthews and Prothro. Pool, Abelson and Popkin report an unusual and interesting effort at simulating the American electorate in *Candidates, Issues and Strategies*.[12] V. O. Key's last book, *The Responsible Electorate*,[13] discusses the reasoned nature of attitudes and behavior in the American public which was one of the concerns of his earlier book, *Public Opinion and American Democracy*.[14]

A comparative analysis of political socialization by Almond and

[5] Angus Campbell *et al.*, *Elections and the Political Order* (New York: John Wiley and Sons, Inc., 1966).

[6] Robert E. Lane, *Political Life* (New York: The Free Press, 1959).

[7] Austin Ranney, *Essays on the Behavioral Study of Politics* (Urbana: University of Illinois Press, 1962).

[8] Heinz Eulau, *The Behavioral Persuasion in Politics* (New York: Random House, 1965).

[9] Edward Dreyer and Walter Rosenbaum, eds., *Political Opinion and Electoral Behavior* (Belmont: Wadsworth Publishing Co., 1966).

[10] Nelson W. Polsby, Robert A. Dentler and Paul A. Smith, *Politics and Social Life: An Introduction to Political Behavior* (Boston: Houghton Mifflin Company, 1963).

[11] Donald Matthews and James Prothro, *Negroes and the New Southern Politics* (New York: Harcourt, Brace and World, Inc., 1967).

[12] Ithiel de Sola Pool, Robert Abelson and Samuel Popkin, *Candidates, Issues and Strategies* (Cambridge: The M.I.T. Press, 1964).

[13] V. O. Key, Jr., *The Responsible Electorate* (Cambridge: Belknap Press, 1966).

[14] V. O. Key, Jr., *Public Opinion and American Democracy* (New York: Alfred A. Knopf, 1961).

Verba, *The Civic Culture*,[15] includes the United States along with four other countries and puts American political behavior in a different perspective, as does Robert Alford's *Party and Society*,[16] a comparative study of voting behavior. There are several theoretical works dealing with public opinion and voting and the most prominent are *An Economic Theory of Democracy*[17] by Anthony Downs and *A Preface to Democratic Theory*[18] by Robert Dahl. *Political Man*[19] by S. M. Lipset covers numerous topics in public opinion and voting behavior, including ideology, which is the central concern of *Political Ideology*[20] by Robert Lane. The work of Herbert McClosky has dealt with ideology and political psychology but as yet appears only in article form.

Not all of the significant studies of American voting behavior have centered around attitudes. V. O. Key demonstrated the applications of the analysis of election returns for describing and understanding political behavior in *American State Politics*,[21] and recently Milton Cummings has written in the same tradition in *Congressmen and the Electorate*.[22] In a few years there will be a practically complete collection of national election returns for major offices recorded by counties and available through the Inter-university Consortium for Political Research. These data will allow more elaborate historical election analysis than heretofore.

By drawing on these studies and data provided through the Inter-university Consortium for Political Research at the University of Michigan, I will summarize the analysis of American political behavior around five major topics. Chapter 1 will explore the characteristics of the electorate during the past 100 years and then concentrate on explanations of non-participation and particularly of non-voting at the present time. In Chapter 2 the broad outlines of partisan political forces are described and the three main categories of American voters,

[15] Gabriel Almond and Sidney Verba, *The Civic Culture* (Princeton, N. J.: Princeton University Press, 1963).

[16] Robert R. Alford, *Party and Society* (Chicago: Rand McNally and Company, 1963).

[17] Anthony Downs, *An Economic Theory of Democracy* (New York: Harper and Brothers, 1957).

[18] Robert A. Dahl, *A Preface to Democratic Theory* (Chicago: University of Chicago Press, 1956).

[19] Seymour M. Lipset, *Political Man* (Garden City, N. Y.: Doubleday and Company, 1960).

[20] Robert E. Lane, *Political Ideology* (New York: The Free Press, 1962).

[21] V. O. Key, Jr., *American State Politics* (New York: Alfred A. Knopf, 1956).

[22] Milton Cummings, *Congressmen and the Electorate* (New York: The Free Press, 1966).

Republicans, Democrats and independents, are discussed. The next chapter investigates the social background of partisans and independents and some of the main social explanations of political behavior are described with an emphasis on primary groups, secondary groups and social class. In Chapter 4 an alternative to social and economic explanations of political behavior, political opinions and ideology is considered, with emphasis on psychological factors. In the final chapter the focus is on political campaigns and the factors which influence the outcome of elections.

In effect, after the initial consideration of suffrage and turnout, the non-participants in the electoral system are dropped from consideration. The two major factors accounting for complete non-participation in civic activities are legal restrictions and apathy, and these two factors are not useful in accounting for more active forms of political behavior. Partisanship is the major determinant of political behavior in the American setting and appears to have far greater impact on vote choice and attitudes than either social class or political ideology. These three elements, partisanship, social class and ideology, suggest the broad outline of explanation of political behavior: during an individual's life, social class and, more generally, social conditions determine ideology and partisanship which mutually influence each other and in turn determine vote choices and positions on political issues. Throughout this dominant pattern of relationships, personality characteristics modify or exaggerate the impact of the main forces at work. Because in American society the social conditions are so varied, the political relationships are not simple and dramatic, but rather present a diffuse pattern of complex interrelationships. These patterns are the focus of subsequent chapters.

There is a complication in the examination of political behavior over a long time. Not only does the electorate shift its policy preference, become more or less liberal, more or less internationalist, but the parties shift as well. If both the parties and the electorate shift as they seemingly have in recent decades, there may be a deceptive stability in voting patterns that conceals a large shift in policy implications. The following analysis ignores political leaders and party platforms while concentrating on the public. The public should be viewed as the background against which Presidents, legislators, and political leaders generally seek public office and make policy. The public not only represents a potential influence on many aspects of the policy-making process but is a persistently interesting political phenomenon quite apart from its implications for the operation of American government.

chapter 1

Suffrage and Turnout

In the united states today over 60 per cent of all adults vote in Presidential elections, and all but a rather small minority of adults are eligible to register to vote if they choose to do so. Widespread participation of all adults in elections and the nearly universal extension of suffrage are fairly recent developments in our political history. During most of the 176 years of American electoral history, a minority of adults have been eligible to vote.

Through the amendments to the United States Constitution, there have been two major extensions of suffrage; in practice and in law there has been a more uneven development.[1] These extensions of suffrage have not been easy or inevitable and I will suggest two factors which account for extensions of suffrage or explain the existence of political forces which bring them about. *In stable political systems the extension of suffrage will result from 1) a widely shared commitment to moral principles which entail further grants of suffrage, and 2) the expectation among political leaders that the newly enfranchised would support their policy preferences.*

The political rhetoric of America carries strong themes of egalitarian democracy, and, normally, young people who go through the political and civic training in the educational system absorb the ideals of individualism and equality. American nationalism, with the myths of the frontier and the melting pot, has justified these values. In part, the goals of American education are participation in and support of American democracy. Although seldom explicitly political in their indoctrina-

---

[1] For a discussion of the legal history of civil rights most American government textbooks will provide a general introduction.

tion, American religious institutions have reinforced these themes in the political culture. American literature and theater contribute to political education in these values. The result is that most Americans have had a commitment to equality, individualism, and democracy, which has provided a basis for support of extensions of voting rights.

To be sure, there have been counter-themes in American political culture. As in any complex society, there are conflicting ideals and perspectives which contradict and undermine one another. It is merely a contention—which will not be proved—that American political culture has been dominated by ideas and beliefs which favored the extension of voting rights and that when suffrage has been restricted it has been treated as an exception to more general political principles. Usually it requires a tremendous effort for a sub-culture to maintain beliefs and values in conflict with the main culture. The Southern way of life can be viewed as sub-culture values and social practices aimed in part at keeping the Negro from being covered by the general beliefs in equality and individual rights. Although successful, the imposition of the Southern sub-culture has entailed great social and psychological costs.

In the two dramatic extensions of suffrage, to Negroes and to women, there have been obvious expectations on the part of political leaders as to what policies the newly enfranchised would support. The Negro voters in the South after the Civil War were one of the mechanisms of anticipated Republican domination of Southern states, and perhaps most Southern states passed through a period where there was at least some chance of combining the votes of Negroes and Populists into a governing majority. The intense prejudice of the whites and difficulty in maintaining the enfranchisement of the Negro kept this strategy an unpromising one under most circumstances, but a significant element in the Republican enthusiasm for Negro suffrage was the knowledge that Republican votes were being added to the rolls.

There was considerable idealism behind the efforts to enfranchise Negroes, and the same idealism appears to have supported suffrage for women. Women were expected to clean up politics once they had the vote; they were seen optimistically as the cure for corruption in government, unwavering opponents of alcohol, and champions of virtue in the electorate. Reformers of all sorts hopefully encouraged the enfranchisement of women as a means of promoting their own goals.

Another aspect of the extension of suffrage in the United States is more uncommon in stable democratic regimes. The addition of states in the frontier expansion across the continent added millions of voters to the electorate throughout the nineteenth century. The vast geographical expansion of the nation kept the electorate overwhelmingly rural. During the decades immediately prior to the Civil War, the politics of slavery dominated the political decisions on additions of states with accompanying expectations as to the policy impact of expansion. To some degree, the extensions of state boundaries amounted to following the nation's electorate westward.

EXTENSIONS OF SUFFRAGE

In the Colonial period and the early years of the Republic, suffrage was commonly restricted to white males with varying amounts of property, so only a proportion of the adult population was eligible to vote. The severity of the impact of the property requirements varied from state to state and their enforcement varied perhaps even more. Gradually the amount of property held or the amount of taxes paid to obtain suffrage was reduced. Sometimes these changes were hard-won reforms enacted by state legislatures or by state constitutional changes, but in other circumstances practical considerations led to substantial reforms. For example, in the Western frontier areas in the nineteenth century, delays in acquiring final title to land holdings made it inexpedient to impose property requirements. Very early in American history in some local elections, candidates would agree among themselves that all white males could vote rather than try to impose complicated restrictions on the electorate. Only in more settled communities can refined restrictions of suffrage be effectively imposed. In sections of the East, powerful landlords controlled the votes of tenants and supported their enfranchisement.[2]

After granting suffrage to white males, the next major change was the enfranchisement of Negroes and subsequently their disfranchisement in the South. We will take up this aspect of American electoral patterns below. The last major extension of voting rights was suffrage for women. As Figure 1.1 illustrates of the extension of suffrage in the United States, the enfranchisement of women was the most dramatic increase in eligible voters. During the years after World War II, only a very small proportion of all adults were not eligible to vote. Throughout American history there have been different state and local election practices which means there is no single set of suffrage requirements which can be used as a basis for deciding exactly who belongs to the electorate at any one time. In fact there were many different electorates with different characteristics.

Although we do not have extensive data on the characteristics of the national electorate during the first century of the Republic, some

[2] Chilton Williamson, *American Suffrage from Property to Democracy 1760–1860* (Princeton: Princeton University Press, 1960), especially pp. 138–81.

FIGURE 1.1
The Proportion of the Adult Population Eligible to Vote, 1860–1960.

Sources: Robert Lane. *Political Life*. (New York: The Free Press of Glencoe, 1959) p. 21; U.S. Bureau of the Census, *Statistical Abstract of the United States: 1965*. (86th edition.) Washington, D.C., 1965, p. 384.

reasonable inferences can be made from the suffrage laws and the descriptive data shown in Figure 1.2. Of course, during the early years of the Republic, almost all voters resided in rural areas and, as Figure 1.2 indicates, the electorate has become steadily more urban over 150 years. By the mid-twentieth century the electorate had become predominantly city and town dwellers. The literacy rate of the electorate was high from the beginning, although the level of education was not. During the nineteenth century, only a very small fraction of Americans graduated from high school. As Figure 1.2 shows, about 2 or 3 per cent of the seventeen-year-olds in a given year graduated from high school in 1870 and 1880, but the rate increased rapidly during the first half of the twentieth century to the point where now about two-thirds of the seventeen-year-olds graduate from high school. When Negroes were enfranchised after the Civil War, only about half of them had recently been slaves but the overwhelming majority were illiterate. The illiteracy rate among Negroes has steadily declined and at the present approaches the very low rate among whites. (The somewhat higher rate among Negroes is mainly the result of illiteracy among older Negroes in the population.) Naturalized citizens have never been a large proportion of the electorate and they are a decreasing feature of the electorate. Additional data would probably show that the peak of

Percent

— % living in rural areas

--- % of seventeen-year-olds graduating from high school

········ % of electorate who are naturalized citizens

—— % illiterate among whites

—·—·— % illiterate among non-whites

FIGURE 1.2.

Estimated Characteristics of the Electorate, 1820–1960.

Source: U.S. Bureau of the Census. *Historical Statistics of the United States, Colonial Times to 1957; Continuation to 1962 and Revisions.* (U.S. Government Printing Office, Washington, D.C., 1965), p. 207, p. 65, p. 9.

naturalized citizens in the electorate never exceeded 25 per cent. For all the unpleasant aspects of the reception and treatment of immigrants, the political system accommodated millions of people from abroad without great stress.

To summarize these data, the voters of 1789 can be described as white male adults who held some property. In the most permissive states, 80 per cent or more of the white male adults may have been eligible to vote; in the most restrictive states, less than 10 per cent were eligible to vote. By 1850 property qualifications still existed in some states, but in many areas restrictions on white males had all but disappeared. After the Civil War, Negroes were added to the electorate and held the franchise for about thirty years when most Negroes were disfranchised. By the early part of the twentieth century, some Negroes enjoyed the vote in certain areas and women had acquired the vote in a variety of types of elections, but the bulk of the electorate were white males. During this period, large numbers of immigrants joined the electorate. After 1920 more and more women joined the electorate, and by 1950 in the North the electorate and the adult population were roughly equivalent. In 1950 in the South, large numbers of women and Negroes were still outside the electorate, but this has changed steadily in recent years.

TURNOUT AND INTEREST

One of two general explanations for participation in elections is that *high turnout is a result of intense competition and strong party organizations.* These two factors are interrelated in so far as competition becomes more intense as strong party organizations make greater and greater efforts to bring in the marginally involved citizens. The other explanation is that *high turnout is a result of greater interest in the electorate; low turnout a result of little interest.* Both explanations have some validity but the second is much better supported by evidence than the first. In recent elections, competition and party organization have had much less impact on turnout than the level of interest in the electorate. The expected relationship between interest, involvement, and information and turnout in elections is shown in Figure 1.3, and this relationship is confirmed by recent data based on survey research in many countries. Presidential elections are high interest and high turnout elections; off-year Congressional elections are moderate interest and moderate turnout elections, and ordinary primary elections are low interest and low turnout elections.

There are two "deviant" cases, contrary to the expected relationship between turnout and interest, and they deserve notice. The first deviant case, labeled "alienation," of high interest and little or no

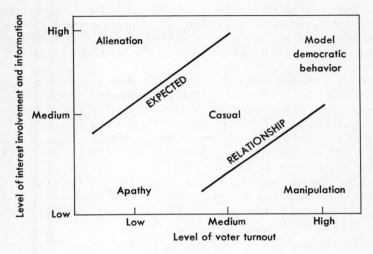

FIGURE 1.3

Hypothetical Relationships between Electoral Turnout and Levels of Interest, Involvement and Information.

turnout may be a situation of voluntary alienation in which individuals withdraw from political participation purposefully. Their high level of interest and information implies they withdraw for some reason; they are dissatisfied with or offended by the political system. "Nonvoluntary alienation" refers to situations in which interested potential voters are prevented from participating. Both situations are dangerous to the political system in that highly interested and informed citizens who refuse to participate have the potential for extremely disruptive activities. So far as we know alienation in this form is very uncommon in American politics.

The second deviant case, low interest and high turnout, labeled "manipulation," refers to a situation in which individuals with little information or interest become involved in voting. Presumably this "manipulation" is achieved by getting individuals to vote either through coercion or by highly stimulating and arousing appeals. Coercive methods for assuring turnout may range from police-state orders to fines for failure to vote. More common in the American political system are exceptionally moving or alarming appeals that bring people to the polls who are so unsophisticated that they are easily moved. It is possible to inspire very high levels of turnout by emotional, inflammatory appeals, and perhaps this happened for many years in the United States after the Civil War. We know campaigns were marked by extreme appeals and we know that there were very high levels of turnout. We cannot be so sure about interest, involvement and information; but since education levels were low, we might reasonably suspect there were lower levels of interest and information than during the twentieth century. We will return to a discussion of this situation below.

We expect the relationship between turnout and interest to account for the lower levels of turnout in Congressional elections or in primary elections as a reflection of lower interest in those elections. More specifically, *we not only expect different levels of interest from one type of election to another but we expect differencs in the level of turnout for any given type of election to vary with the amount of interest in that particular race.*

A number of elements would seem to influence the amount of interest in an election. The differences in levels of interest from Presidential elections to Congressional elections to primary elections can be viewed as a result of:

1) differences in media coverage given the election;
2) significance attached by voters to the office;
3) importance of issues raised in the campaign;
4) attractiveness of candidates.

Variation in these factors leads to what Angus Campbell has called "high stimulus" and "low stimulus" elections.[3]

Newspapers and television give far more coverage to the activities and speeches of Presidential candidates than to Congressional candidates. Even the most indifferent citizen comes to possess impressions and some information about Presidential candidates and their campaign. This bombardment through the mass media awakens the relatively uninterested and often provides them with some reason for bothering to vote. This is not nearly so likely to happen in other election campaigns where only the motivated citizens will become informed and concerned to any degree. Even so, a week or so after the election, a substantial proportion of the voters will not recall the name of the Congressional candidate for whom they voted.

The outcome of elections in the United States is not viewed as desperately serious by most voters. There is an easygoing attitude toward most contests and a feeling that it does not matter greatly who wins. Few elections take on great significance for many voters, but there are exceptions. In 1960, for instance, throughout the country some Protestants became concerned over the threat of a Catholic in the White House; for some voters concern over the outcome became intense. Sometimes issues are raised which stimulate interest and concern in the electorate. In 1964 some voters apparently responded with

[3] Angus Campbell *et al., Elections and the Political Order* (New York: John Wiley and Sons, Inc., 1966), pp. 40–62.

concern to the "trigger-happy" image of Goldwater, but it is difficult to point to dramatic instances of large numbers of voters being much concerned with a particular issue. Voters may respond to attractive qualities in the candidates. The Eisenhower elections of 1952 and 1956 seem to have offered a candidate attractive enough to motivate otherwise indifferent people to vote, and the same thing happens occasionally in local elections. Still these four factors, media coverage, importance of the office, issue salience and attractive candidates, are more likely to be present in a high degree in a Presidential election than in lesser races, even though exceptional local races might be strong on all four. This general tendency means that Presidential elections are much more likely to be "high stimulus" elections with high turnout and other elections are likely to be "low stimulus" elections with lighter voting.

TURNOUT IN AMERICAN ELECTIONS

Surely one of the most persistent complaints about the American electoral system is its failure in the twentieth century to achieve the high rates of voter turnout found in other countries and common in this country in the nineteenth century. Democracies around the world frequently record turnout rates over 90 per cent while turnout in the United States exceeds 60 per cent only in Presidential elections. The unfavorable comparisons are misleading on several grounds, since turnout is computed in different ways in each country. In most foreign countries, rates of turnout are based on lists of registered voters rather than on the total eligible electorate or the adult population. There are no detailed comparative studies of voting but the reported rates exaggerate turnout perhaps by 15 per cent or more. The rates of turnout in the United States, on the other hand, usually fail to take into account the substantial limitations on eligibility associated with residence requirements and other restrictions. The most careful estimate of American turnout takes into account all the various restrictions and concludes that turnout in the 1960 Presidential election was over 80 per cent of the eligible electorate.[4] This rate is about 20 per cent higher than the "official" rate in Figure 1.4, but for the convenience of comparison with other years I will use the lower rates in the following discussion.

While suffrage was extended during the past 100 years, there was a decline in the proportion of eligible voters turning out for elections, as shown in Figure 1.4. With each extension of suffrage—and most dramatically the enfranchisement of women in 1920—there is a substantial drop in the proportion voting. During the nineteenth century

[4] William G. Andrews, "American Voting Participation," *The Western Political Quarterly*, Vol. XIX (1966), p. 639.

FIGURE 1.4
*Estimated Turnout of Eligible Voters in the South and Non-South,
1860–1964.*

Sources: Robert Lane. *Political Life.* (New York: The Free Press of Glencoe,
1959) p. 20; U.S. Bureau of the Census. *Statistical Abstract of the United
States:* 1965. (86th edition.) Washington, D.C., 1965. p. 384; Walter Dean
Burnham, "The Changing Shape of the American Political Universe," *American
Political Science Review,* Vol. LIX (March, 1965) p. 11, Figure 1.

national turnout appears extremely high—always over 70 per cent.
The decline in national turnout in Figure 1.4 from shortly before 1900
to 1916 is associated with the restriction of Negro voting in the South,
but this factor does not explain the decline in turnout found elsewhere.
This decline in voting also results from the increasing one-party domination of the South, since the absence of party competition there resulted
in far lower turnout than can be accounted for by the disfranchisement
of Negroes alone.

The effective disfranchisement of Negroes (and many low-income
whites) was accomplished at different times in the states of the old
Confederacy, but generally the severe limitations of the electorate did
not occur until late in the nineteenth century or shortly after the turn
of the twentieth century. Several techniques for disfranchising Negroes
have been used during the past century in the South and from time to
time some of these techniques have been applied in the North on a
more limited basis to restrict the electoral participation of immigrants.

The most common methods have been the poll tax, literacy tests, white primaries, discriminatory administrative procedures, and intimidation. It would be extremely difficult to state precisely what impact these techniques have had at various times, but a few general observations can be made. The Negroes' low social and economic circumstances surely contribute to non-participation since these conditions lead to low interest and non-participation elsewhere and among all groups. Furthermore, in many parts of the South Negroes are offered only anti-Negro candidates to support—a condition not likely to inspire voter participation.

A study of Negro registration in 1958 by Matthews and Prothro[5] indicated that Southern states using poll taxes and literacy tests inhibited Negro voter registration. The now-illegal poll tax, a flat fee charged each individual as a prerequisite for registration to vote, was used for many years and no doubt disfranchised both poor Negroes and poor whites. It has become less effective in recent years as well as unpopular with the white voters who have had to pay it while the Negro, disfranchised by other means, has not paid it. The literacy test has given local officials a device which could be administered in a selective way to permit registration of whites and practically prohibit the registration of Negroes. The "standards of literacy" applied in some cases to Negroes have precluded registration. Similar administrative devices have blocked the attempts of Negroes to register. To remain effective over long periods of time these devices probably have depended on the threat or use of violence against Negroes.

Matthews and Prothro also demonstrate that competitive factions within the Democratic Party are associated with increased Negro registration while competition between Republicans and Democrats is not. In addition, the existence of Negro political and civil rights organizations in a county are associated with increased registration. Surprisingly, in the 1950's incidents of racial violence do not appear to be associated with Negro registration; that is, high levels of violence do not substantially reduce registration. This does not mean that intimidation is ineffective or the violence serves no purpose, but there is no simple relationship between violence and registration.

The Northern states in Figure 1.4 present a more difficult problem in explanation since there is a substantial decline in turnout in the first two decades of the twentieth century, and turnout has not returned to its previous levels. The disfranchisement of Negroes and whites found in the South cannot account for Northern non-voting. There are two quite different explanations of the decline in voting in the North commencing in the late 1890's.

[5] Donald R. Matthews and James W. Prothro, "Political Factors and Negro Voter Registration in the South," *American Political Science Review*, Vol. LVII (June, 1963), pp. 355–67.

A persuasive case has been made by Schattschneider[6] and Burnham[7] in their studies of this period. Basically, they contend that there was a high level of party loyalty and political involvement during the late nineteenth century, causing high turnout and great partisan stability. Sometime during the 1890's electoral patterns shifted in such a way that the South became safely Democratic and most of the rest of the nation came under the domination of the Republican Party. Schattschneider's analysis emphasizes the degree to which this alignment enabled conservatives in both regions to dominate American politics for many years. A consequence of declining competition and greater conservatism throughout the electoral system, according to this line of argument, is a loss of interest in politics accompanied by lower turnout and less partisan loyalty. Burnham emphasizes the disintegration of party voting with more ticket splitting and lower turnout in off-year elections.

Some elements of this account are undeniable. There was a shift in electoral patterns after 1896 with much of the nation changing from competitive to one-party areas. Throughout areas previously characterized by high turnout, straight ticket voting, and stable voting patterns, there were greater fluctuations in turnout and partisan stability.

An alternative set of arguments is consistent with these patterns but gives them a different interpretation. The high rate of turnout may not have been a result of political involvement by an interested, well-informed electorate, but on the contrary may have been possible at all only because of low levels of information and interest. A largely uninformed electorate was aroused to vote by means of extreme and emotional political appeals. Presumably these alarming bits of information in the absence of a more general awareness of what was at stake produced firm commitments to vote. But by and large the parties manipulated the electorate and this manipulation was possible because the electorate was not well-informed. Currently in Europe it is correct to say that the higher the interest in and information on politics in the nation generally, the lower the turnout in elections.

Furthermore the party organization "delivered" or "voted" substantial numbers of voters during this period. The remarkable stability of party voting during this period may be a testimony to the corruption of the party organizations. The decline of stable party voting in the early twentieth century coincides with various attacks on political

---

[6] E. E. Schattschneider. *The Semisovereign People* (New York: Holt, Rinehart and Winston, 1960), esp. chap. 5.

[7] Walter Dean Burnham, "The Changing Shape of the American Political Universe," *American Political Science Review*, Vol. LIX (March, 1965), pp. 7–28.

corruption and party machines. In fact, the apparent hostility in the
electorate to the parties throughout this period seems inconsistent with
extremely high levels of party loyalty.

The decline in turnout outside the South in subsequent elections
may have resulted from the failure of the Democratic Party to offer a
sufficiently attractive alternative to draw votes away from the Republicans, who had the advantage of being associated with prosperity and a
military victory. Republican dominance was not broken until another
depression, except for elections of 1912 and 1916 when the Republicans
were divided. The early decades of the twentieth century brought the
decline of party machines and increased honesty in electoral activities,
both of which could have reduced turnout.

Turnout in national elections, as shown in Figure 1.5, has generally increased in the past forty-five years with the exception of the
World War II years and immediately thereafter. There are great
differences in turnout among the states concealed within these national
data. As Figure 1.4 shows, there are consistently low rates of voting
in the South; turnout in Northern states runs around ten percentage
points above the national average. The most consistent pattern in Figure
1.5 reveals that in non-Presidential election years there is always a
decline in turnout. Even in a Presidential year fewer people vote in
Congressional elections, but the dramatic decline in turnout is the 10
to 20 per cent decline in voting in the off-year elections. It is reasonable
to expect the differences in turnout between North and South to
disappear gradually as competition increases, but the different rates of

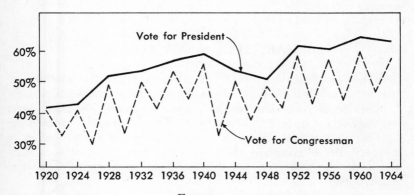

FIGURE 1.5
*Turnout of Eligible Voters in Presidential and Congressional
Elections, 1920–1964.*

Source: U.S. Bureau of the Census. *Statistical Abstract of the United States:*
1965. (86th edition.) Washington, D.C., 1965. p. 384.

voting in Presidential and Congressional elections are more likely to endure.

Since we have postulated that turnout is in part a function of competition, we might expect the more competitive primary elections in Southern states to have a higher rate of participation than general elections dominated by the Democrats. In general this does indeed appear to be the case, but the level of turnout is still about half the higher rates of voting in the North. Apparently the competition in Southern primaries has not had sufficient impact on the political mood of the South to alter basic attitudes toward participation in elections.

There are other variables related to turnout, as Figure 1.6 shows. Both age and level of education are related to turnout, but we know that these variables are also related to interest in politics. For example, both young people and old people are less interested in politics and campaigns than middle-aged people. College-educated individuals have a higher level of interest; grade school-educated a lower level of interest. Men are more interested in politics than women. Individuals with higher incomes show more interest than lower-income individuals. These relationships between turnout and characteristics like age, education, income, and region appear to hold for all elections in much the same way. The more important observation, however, is that the distribution of these personal characteristics for non-voters and voters are about the same in all elections. This means that about the same proportion of non-voters are over sixty-five or have a college education in a Presidential election or an off-year election. *The social composition of voters and non-voters does not change significantly from one election to the next.*

HABITUAL NON-VOTERS

Over the years, most Americans vote at least occasionally. The fluctuations in turnout bring different individuals to the polls at each election. A rather small proportion of the potential national electorate never votes, about 15 per cent in recent years. These, habitual non-voters are distinctly unlike those citizens who vote, but most of the non-voters in any particular election are individuals who have voted at least occasionally in the past. We will now turn our attention to these non-participants.

Almost half of the habitual non-voters live in the South. Over two-thirds of these non-participants are women; one-fourth are Negro. They are disproportionately poor; 22 per cent live in households with incomes under $2,000 in 1964 and the next 35 per cent with incomes between $3,000 and $5,000—about twice the rate of low incomes as the rest of

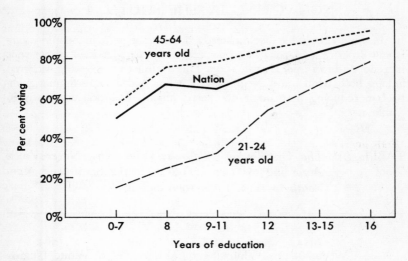

FIGURE 1.6
*Turnout in the 1964 Presidential Election
According to Age and Education.*

Source: U.S. Bureau of the Census. *Current Population Reports*, Series P-20,
No. 143, "Voter Participation in the National Election: November 1964,"
U.S. Government Printing Office, Washington, D.C., 1965. p. 16.

the population. About half are young—under thirty—so they have passed
up only a few opportunities to vote. One-third have a grade school
education or less, and over 60 per cent live in working class households.
This group as a whole has very little interest in politics; over 50 per
cent expressed no interest at all in the 1964 campaign and 50 per cent
said that they cared very little or not at all whether Johnson or Goldwater won the Presidency. As a group they are unlikely to have opinions
on matters of public policy.

Outside the South in the last fifteen years this group of non-voters
has remained constant in size, around 7 or 8 per cent of the electorate.
Individuals are constantly leaving this category by voting in an election,
for by age forty virtually everyone outside the South eligible to vote
has voted at least occasionally. The non-voters in the North come from
two main sources: young people entering the electorate who do not
vote initially, and disfranchised Negroes from the South who do not
vote immediately in the North because of residence requirements or
for some other reason.

NON-VOTING IN THE SOUTH

In the South there has been a steady decrease of permanent non-voters from 38 per cent in 1952 to 26 per cent four years later, to 18 per cent in 1960, and to 15 per cent in 1964. This decline in non-voting occurred among both whites and Negroes, but it has had a more dramatic impact in reducing permanent non-voters among Negroes, as shown in Table 1.1.

TABLE 1.1　*The Distribution of Adults Who Have Never Voted According to Race and Sex for the South and Non-South in 1952, 1956, 1960 and 1964.*

| | SOUTH[a] | | | | | | | |
| | 1952 | | 1956 | | 1960 | | 1964 | |
	White	Negro	White	Negro	White	Negro	White	Negro
Men	12%	65%	14%	60%	8%	33%	5%	26%
	(131)[c]	(48)	(200)	(30)	(228)	(39)	(156)	(31)
Women	33%	87%	27%	70%	17%	63%	14%	39%
	(193)	(61)	(230)	(53)	(332)	(56)	(357)	(90)
	NON-SOUTH[b]							
Men	6%	17%	6%	17%	6%	11%	7%	10%
	(516)	(23)	(527)	(29)	(576)	(38)	(435)	(20)
Women	7%	11%	10%	32%	7%	28%	7%	18%
	(574)	(27)	(649)	(41)	(633)	(39)	(499)	(48)

　　[a] The states included in the "South" are: Alabama, Arkansas, Florida, Georgia, Kentucky, Louisiana, Maryland, Mississippi, North Carolina, Oklahoma, South Carolina, Tennessee, Texas, Virginia, West Virginia.
　　[b] The states included in the "Non-South" are the remainder.
　　[c] The numbers in parentheses are the numbers of individuals interviewed who fall into each category.
Source: Survey Research Center, University of Michigan.

　　Substantial proportions of Negroes still have never voted in the South, but the change from 1952 to 1964 is impressive, and a large proportion of Southern women, both white and Negro, had never voted in a Presidential election as recently as 1952. In the South there is a persistent tendency for non-voting to be higher among women regardless of race just as non-voting is higher among Negroes regardless of sex. It is not possible from these data to infer how many of these Southern Negroes would have participated in a political culture that was more receptive to their activity. It is obvious that Southern Negroes, say in 1952, were not engaged in politics up to thèir potential, since their rate of participation increased in the following years far more rapidly than any change in the level of education and income among Negroes.[8]

During recent years there has been a dramatic change in the political involvement of Southern Negroes as shown in Figure 1.7. In 1952 when most Southern Negroes had never voted and before the major symbolic events like Little Rock or the demonstrations, the Southern whites had a higher level of interest in politics than Negroes even allowing for educational differences. For the next twelve years, there was an awakening of interest and concern among Negroes, resulting by 1964 in a higher level of interest than among whites at each level of education.

To some extent, non-voting Southern Negroes are a special case representing the only sizable bloc of potential voters in the American electorate who are prevented from participating. But a more general explanation of habitual non-voting also applied to this group for many years: *deprived social conditions or inhibiting cultural values lead to low interest in, little concern with, and little information on politics and that in turn leads to non-voting.*

YOUTHFUL NON-VOTERS

Another group of non-voters forming about 8 per cent of the electorate is the young people who pass up their first opportunities to vote. Figure 1.6 shows the tendency of young people not to vote in the first election for which they are eligible regardless of their level of education. Young people are somewhat less interested in politics than older citizens, but among non-voters young people are more interested in and concerned with politics than older non-voters, as we might expect from their higher level of education. Although there is considerable popular attention given to youthful rebellion, most young people

[8] For the most sophisticated analysis of the political behavior of Southern Negroes see the recent study by Matthews and Prothro, *Negroes and the New Southern Politics, op cit.* In the current literature see D. R. Matthews and J. W. Prothro, "Southern Racial Attitudes: Conflict, Awareness and Political Change," *The Annals of the American Academy of Political and Social Science,* CCCXLIV (November, 1962), pp. 108–21, and "The Concept of Party Image and Its Importance for the Southern Electorate," in M. K. Jennings and L. H. Zeigler, *The Electoral Process* (Englewood Cliffs, N. J.: Prentice-Hall, Inc., 1966), pp. 139–74.

FIGURE 1.7
*Interest in Politics Among Southern Whites and Negroes
According to Education, 1952, 1964.*

Source: Survey Research Center, University of Michigan.

and most older Americans, for that matter, follow the political voting patterns of their parents. Most young people learn to identify with a political party a number of years before they are old enough to vote, and most commonly they follow the party of their parents. Among these new members of the electorate, only 7 per cent report they have switched away from the party of their fathers to the other party; 68 per cent are identified with the same party and 24 per cent have switched to or continued an independent status. These findings support the generalizations originally documented for a single community by Maccoby, Matthews and Morton.[9]

Among young people, women are as likely to vote as men, although this characteristic may result from the unsettled circumstances of many young men. Military service, new jobs, the last years of college all

---

[9] See E. E. Maccoby, R. E. Matthews and A. S. Morton, "Youth and Political Change," *Public Opinion Quarterly*, Vol. 18 (1954), pp. 23–29, for one of the few studies devoted to this topic.

contribute to postponing the establishment of residence, and the initiation of political participation.

Democrats far outnumber Republicans among new voters, since for thirty years new voters have identified with Democrats by two to one or more. Even though 1964 is the most extremely Democratic year among new voters of any election since 1936, the following distributions are only slightly more Democratic than those during the 1950's. In 1964 53 per cent identified with the Democratic Party in contrast with 16 per cent identified with the Republican Party. Almost one-third consider themselves independents. This means that in terms of the total electorate there has been a net gain of 2 per cent to the Democrats about every four years caused by young people entering the electorate with pro-Democratic sympathies.

Although several exceptions have appeared, the basic proposition remains that in the American electorate high turnout is associated with high interest, involvement and information. The disfranchisement of Southern Negroes is the clearest case of coerced non-participation in American electoral history. Young people may offer an example of fairly interested potential voters who are frequently prevented from voting by residential mobility and inconvenience. But for most Americans electoral turnout in all types of elections is related to interest and concern.

chapter 2

Partisans and Independents

GENERALLY OF GREATER INTEREST THAN TURNOUT ARE PARTISAN VOTING patterns and the division of votes between Democrats and Republicans. Preferences for candidates vary greatly over the years and within elections between Democrats and Republicans. In some constituencies the variation of support in a single election will create "landslides" for candidates of both parties caused by substantial numbers of voters "splitting their tickets," that is, voting for candidates from more than one party in a single election. In 1964 over a third of all voters split their ticket for at least one race. *While under the right circumstances American voters have demonstrated the capacity for highly selective and differentiated support for the candidates offered them by the political parties, under most circumstances the majority of voters cast their votes for the candidates of a single party.*

VARIATION

The variation in partisan preference is even greater over the years with most voters occasionally deviating from their customary choices. If we consider only a single race like the Presidential contest over time, we find that more than a third of the electorate has voted for Presidential candidates from different parties. In recent years the aggregate vote totals for national elections shown in Figure 2.1 reveal a wide range of Democratic fortunes from a low of 42 per cent for Stevenson in his second try against Eisenhower to a high of 61 per cent for Johnson against Goldwater in 1964. The Congressional elections during the thirty-year period illustrated in Figure 2.1 do not indicate the same

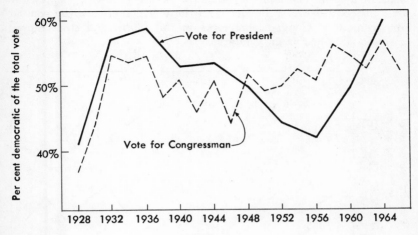

FIGURE 2.1
Presidential and Congressional Votes, 1928–1966.

While presenting these data I have not bothered to draw attention to the wide range of errors that may exist. There are errors in collecting and recording data as well as errors in computation. The presidential election of 1960 provides an illustration of another form of uncertainty that enters into these data and that is choices made among alternative ways of presenting the data. It is customary to list the popular vote in such a way that Kennedy appears a narrow winner over Nixon in 1960. Actually in order to reach this distribution of the total vote it is necessary to exaggerate the Kennedy vote from Alabama since on the slate of Democratic electors in Alabama there were uncommitted electors. Eventually six of the uncommitted electors voted for Harry Byrd and five electors voted for Kennedy. If the Kennedy popular vote in Alabama is reduced to a proportion, say 5/11 in this case, of the vote for Democratic electors and if only this reduced popular vote is added to his national total, Nixon, not Kennedy, has the larger popular vote total nationally in 1960. In percentages these are negligible changes, but symbolically such differences can become important. In these tables I have followed the usual practice of presenting the augmented Kennedy total.

Sources: U.S. Bureau of the Census. *Statistical Abstract of the United States: 1965.* (86th edition) Washington, D.C., 1965; U.S. Bureau of the Census. *Historical Statistics of the United States, Colonial Times to 1957: Continuation to 1962 and Revisions.* (U.S. Government Printing Office, Washington, D.C., 1965); *Congressional Quarterly Weekly Report*, Vol. XXIV (1966) no. 45, p. 2809.

degree of severe fluctuation nor is the path of Democratic percentages in Congressional elections closely associated with the Presidential elections. Figure 2.2 illustrates the important role played by the South in Democratic Party victories. The great advantage enjoyed there by the Democrats in Congressional elections gave them a lead of about 110 seats in the biennial contest for control of the House of Representatives in recent decades; the Democrats have frequently lost the popular vote contest in Congressional races in the North and still enjoyed a comfortable margin in Congress.

FIGURE 2.2
Democratic Vote for Congressman, North and South, 1936–1966.

Source: Same as Figure 2.1.

Figure 2.1 also illustrates the tendency of a victorious party in a Presidential election to do less well in the following Congressional election. From the Congressional vote in the Republican Presidential years of 1952 and 1956 we find an increase in the Democratic vote in 1954 and 1958. All the other Presidential elections in Figure 2.1 were Democratic victories and in each succeeding Congressional election the Republican gained votes.

In analyzing Presidential and Congressional election data it is common to regard the Congressional vote as reflective of the underlying strength of the parties. The Republicans enjoyed a comeback in popularity in the late thirties and through much of the forties—a popularity which was not reflected in Presidential victories. During the fifties when the Republicans won the Presidency, their general strength in the electorate reflected through Congressional elections was declining.[1] Public opinion findings shown in Table 2.1 suggest the same pattern.

[1] Philip Converse and the staff of the Survey Research Center have dealt with the problem of "normal" vote in a far more sophisticated way employing party identification. For explanation of this technique see A. Campbell, *et al.*, *Elections and the Political Order* (New York: John Wiley and Sons, Inc., 1966), pp. 9–39.

A somewhat different way of looking at this phenomenon follows from a comparison of the two lines in Figure 2.3. The voting behavior of independents in Figure 2.3 shows how much they switch from election to election in their net impact of support of each party's candidates. We can also observe from this table that in most Presidential

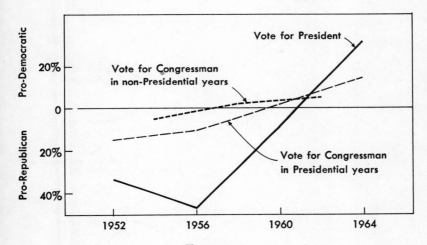

FIGURE 2.3
Net Advantage in Presidential and Congressional
Voting Among Independents, 1952–1964.

Source: Survey Research Center, University of Michigan.

elections the independents swing strongly to one side or the other, and this is one manifestation of the short-run forces at work in the electorate which benefit one candidate. Independents do not switch their support in Congressional elections as shown in Figure 2.3 nearly as much as they do in Presidential elections. Beyond that we should note in non-Presidential election years there is still less shifting in the net impact of independents' voting.

COMPETITIVENESS IN DISTRICTS

In Figure 2.4 there are several hypothetical distributions of the Democratic percentages in different types of elections, Democratic and Republican landslides, and a closely contested election. Line 1S-2S-3S illustrates the possibility of a district which remains safe no matter how the national tides flow. Line 1D-2D-3D illustrates those districts which are Democratic except in strong Republican years when they are closely competitive; line 1R-2R-3R shows the same situation on the Republican side—a district safe for Republicans except in strong Democratic years. Line 1C-2C-3C shows a district which is competitive under all circumstances. *Competitive districts shift support from parties constantly,*

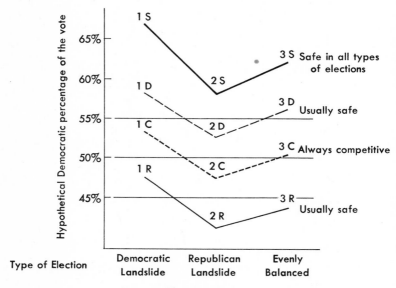

FIGURE 2.4
Patterns of Voting Behavior in Different Types of Elections.

and although the magnitude of variation in these districts may not be greater than in others, they cause elections to be won and lost. For this reason, small shifts in highly competitive districts may loom far more significant to politicians and journalists than much larger variations in safer constituencies. Obviously this illustration applies to states as the units in the electoral college, to Congressional districts or to local constituencies.

The general tendency of constituencies to shift in the same direction should not be overemphasized. In every election some constituencies will move against the tide for special local reasons like an unusually strong or weak candidate or some exceptional issue. In a few elections large numbers of constituencies may move in opposite directions. Recently many Southern constituencies have moved in a Republican direction while the rest of the nation was voting more Democratic.

There is no agreed definition of "competitive," but sophisticated analysis takes into account the frequency of changeover from one party to another. A simpler definition is the winning margin in a single election. A highly competitive race is one in which the winner has less than 52 per cent of the vote and the loser more than 48 per cent. A marginal race is one in which the winner has less than 55 per cent and the loser has more than 45 per cent. More one-sided races are considered landslides or safe districts. *About one-half of Congressional districts in the United States remain safe for one party through both Democratic and Republican years.* In a single year, 1962, less than 20 per cent of the races for the House of Representatives were competitive (that is, had a close election) and in 1964 about 25 per cent were competitive. In 1964, 45 per cent of United States Senate races were competitive, but this appears to be an atypically high rate for competitiveness, with most years having less than 40 per cent of the contests closer than 55 to 45 per cent. Furthermore, the amount of variation is not constant from district to district. Some districts appear immune to the forces influencing other districts, while some fluctuate so much that they appear safely Democratic in one election and safely Republican in another. Another source of variation to be considered below is the difference in turnout from one election to the next.

TURNOUT AND VOTING REGULARITY

A most significant correlate of interest in politics is partisanship and this relationship produces an important characteristic of national voting patterns. We have observed above that usually the party that lost the previous Presidential election gains in Congress in off-year elections. The most straightforward explanation of this regular phenomenon is that *Presidential elections with the accompanying high level of interest draw large numbers of weak partisans and independents to the polls.* These weak partisans and independents are more easily shifted from one party to another—they add disproportionately to the vote for one Presidential candidate—usually the winner. *In Congressional elections these less committed voters do not turn out and disproportionately large numbers of intense partisans vote in these less salient elections.* These strong party identifiers are not as likely to shift their vote away from their party as are other voters. Consequently in Congressional elections there is a decline in the support for the party that had disproportionately large numbers of less interested voters in the previous Presidential elections.

Figure 2.5 illustrates the expected variation in turnout among partisans and independents for different types of elections for "normal" constituencies. In Presidential elections with very high turnout there

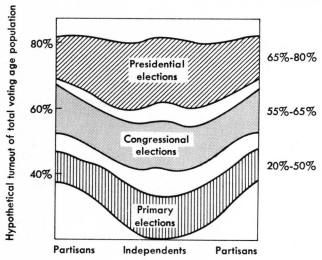

FIGURE 2.5
*Expected Turnout of Partisans and Independents
in Different Types of Elections.*

is little variation along the partisanship dimension, but in less salient Presidential elections like 1948 with Truman and Dewey there will be lower turnout among the less involved. In the most hotly contested Congressional elections there will be high turnout among strong partisans and somewhat less turnout among the weak partisans and independents. In low interest Congressional elections there are greater differences in turnout. Primary elections still further exaggerate this tendency. In all elections the voters near the center represent a more shiftable group, voters more likely to shift for an attractive candidate or over an important issue.[2]

PARTISAN STABILITY

The discussion of voting to this point has emphasized variation, but the stable element in vote choice is equally important. During the past twenty years while there have been landslide elections for both

[2] These phenomena are discussed more thoroughly in Angus Campbell, *et al., Elections and the Political Order*, pp. 40–62.

parties in Presidential and Congressional elections, party loyalty has remained almost unchanged. The general sympathy for and identification with the two political parties has shown remarkably little fluctuation during this period of considerable shifting in aggregate voting behavior.

Table 2.1 presents public opinion survey results from 1940 to 1964. By 1947 the present pattern of partisan preferences is established while prior to that the shift away from the Republican Party occurred. (The 1940 and 1944 percentages for the Republicans appear somewhat exaggerated and the "apoliticals" underestimated.) Presumably this erosion of Republican strength began in the late 1920's and continued with some variation through the thirties, but there are no survey data from that period to document this shifting for individuals. There are two sources of minor variation during this recent period of stability; one is the increase in numbers of Democrats and the other is the further decline in Republican strength. The basic distribution shows that the Democrats and Republicans were almost evenly balanced in the early forties. (With the lower level of turnout among Democrats this would lead to a Republican advantage in normal vote such as we observed in the Congressional elections of 1942 and 1946.) The distribution of the last fifteen years, however, shows a clear advantage to the Democrats with only slightly less than 50 per cent of the electorate as Democrats and slightly over one-fourth as Republicans.

PARTISANSHIP

The pioneer studies in voting behavior ignored partisanship because the early emphasis was on social variables like religion and occupation. Since the first major study by Angus Campbell and his colleagues at the Survey Research Center in 1952,[3] party identification has assumed a central role in all voting behavior analysis. Party identification is a relatively uncomplicated measure which arrays responses to the following questions:

"Generally speaking, do you usually think of yourself as a Republican, a Democrat, an Independent, or what? Would you call yourself a strong (R) (D) or a not very strong (R) (D)?"

Strong Democrat
Democrat
Independent
Republican
Strong Republican

[3] Angus Campbell, Gerald Gurin and Warren Miller, *The Voter Decides* (Evanston: Row, Peterson and Co., 1954).

TABLE 2.1 The Party Identification of the Electorate, 1940–1964.

	1940	1944	1947	1952	1954	1956	1958	1960	1962	1964
Democrats	41%	41%	45%	47%	47%	44%	47%	46%	47%	51%
Independents	20	20	21	22	22	24	19	23	23	22
Republicans	38	39	27	27	27	29	29	27	27	24
Nothing, Don't Know	1	*	2	4	4	3	5	4	3	2
Total	100%	100%	101%	100%	100%	100%	100%	100%	100%	99%
n =[a]	?	?	1287	1614	1139	1772	1269	3021	1317	1571
	(Gallup)		(NORC)	(Survey			Research			Center)

[a] In this table and most of those which follow, the number of individuals interviewed is given underneath the total percentage for the column. In each table the "n's" give the number of individuals who are represented by the percentages in the column above. In this table the "n's" represent the total sample sizes of many studies, but in most tables the "n's" will represent subsets of a single sample.

Sources: National Opinion Research Center; Survey Research Center, University of Michigan; George Gallup, The Political Almanac, 1952 (New York: Forbes, 1952) p. 37; A. Campbell et al., Elections and the Political Order, p. 13.

This self-identification measure of party loyalty is the best indicator of partisanship, and political analysts commonly refer to partisanship and party identification interchangeably. *Partisanship is the most important single influence on political opinions and voting behavior.* Many other influences are at work on voters in our society but none compare in significance with partisanship.[4]

Partisanship represents the feeling of sympathy for and loyalty to a political party an individual acquires (probably) during childhood and which endures (usually) with increasing intensity through his life. Most individuals think of themselves as something politically and this self-image of oneself as a Democrat or a Republican is useful to the individual in a special way. An individual who thinks of himself as a Republican, for example, responds to political information in part by using his party identification to orient himself, to react to new information in such a way that it fits in with the ideals and feelings he already has. A Republican who hears a policy advocated by a Republican Party leader has a basis in his party loyalty for supporting the policy quite apart from other considerations. Or a Democrat may feel favorably toward a candidate for office because he discovers that he is the Democratic candidate. Partisanship may orient the individual in his political environment, but it may also distort his picture of reality.

In order to refine slightly the categories of party identifiers shown in Table 2.1 in the following analysis, the individuals who have never voted are eliminated from the partisan and independent categories. This does not alter substantially the overall composition of the electorate as illustrated by Table 2.1, but it does change the characteristics of the groups by setting apart the habitual non-voters. This yields five categories of active participants in the electorate according to intensity of partisanship as follows:

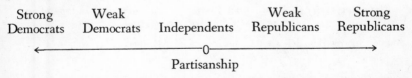

The partisans, strong Democrats and strong Republicans, are loyal to their party and likely to vote in all elections. The sympathizers, weak Democrats and weak Republicans, are less likely to vote and more likely to desert their party occasionally for the other party. The independents have little or no loyalty to either party.

Figure 2.6 shows how these categories of voters behave in Presidential elections according to the findings of the four major Survey

[4] The most important work on party identification is in Angus Campbell *et al.*, *The American Voter* (New York: John Wiley and Sons, Inc., 1960), pp. 120–67.

Research Center surveys. Strong Democratic and Republican partisans report a high degree of loyalty to their party's candidates over the years; naturally almost no partisans have consistently voted for the other party and relatively few have ever switched. The independents on the other hand seldom vote consistently for one party—over 50 per cent reporting in all surveys that they have voted for Presidential candidates from both parties.

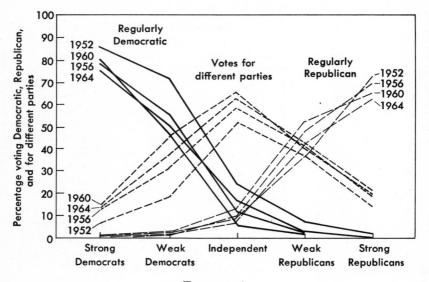

FIGURE 2.6
Party Regularity in Presidential Voting for Partisans and Independents in 1952, 1956, 1960 and 1964.

Source: Survey Research Center, University of Michigan.

Figure 2.7 shows another pattern of voting behavior among partisans and independents in the Presidential elections of 1952, 1956, 1960 and 1964. Overwhelmingly strong partisans support the candidate of their party although there are obviously differences in the appeal of candidates. Eisenhower received exceptionally large proportions of the vote in all categories from most Republican to most Democratic and Goldwater received exceptionally low proportions of the vote in all categories. The turnout varies somewhat in Presidential elections and reveals a slight tendency for the weak partisans to stay at home and a slight tendency for Democrats to stay at home more than the Republicans. (If individuals who never vote were added to these figures, the

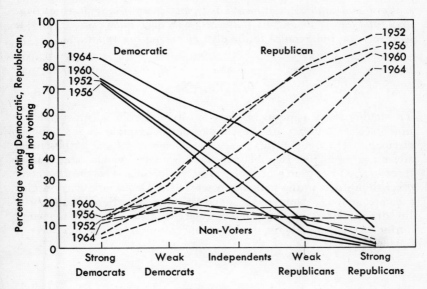

FIGURE 2.7
*Vote for President by Partisans and Independents
in 1952, 1956, 1960 and 1964.*

Source: Survey Research Center, University of Michigan.

Democrats would appear to have even more non-voters; more habitual non-voters consider themselves Democrats than Republicans.)

In the perspective of party strategy these categories of voters must be approached with different purposes in mind. A party has these aims for the respective groups:

VOTER CATEGORY	PARTY STRATEGY
Partisans and sympathizers of the party	—hold their votes and maximize turnout
Independents	—try to win their support
Partisans and sympathizers of the opposition	—try to win their support or appeal to them enough to reduce their turnout
Habitual non-voters	—recruit new voters from potential supporters

It is difficult in practice to isolate these groups and apply a narrow strategy to one type of voter alone. Since political campaigners use appeals that are more or less appropriate for everyone it might be more correct to say that a general campaign approach is hoped to have rather dissimilar results in different categories of voters. By making the party's platform and candidates attractive the party intends to improve turnout and fund-raising among its followers, win over independents, and at least increase indifference to the choices among the opposition.

PARTISANS

The highly stable patterns of party loyalty and political independence in Tables 2.2 and 2.3 are the basis of our description of the national electorate. Throughout this time, the Democrats hold a substantial advantage over the Republicans—an advantage which ranges from three to two in 1956 to a high of two to one in 1964. This means among other things that in the nation as a whole the Democratic Party begins a campaign with many more supporters than the Republican Party. Broadly speaking, the Democrats must try to *hold onto* their following during a campaign while the Republicans must try to *win over* a following.

TABLE 2.2   *The Distribution of Partisans and Independents in 1952, 1956, 1960 and 1964.*

	1952	1956	1960	1964
Strong Democrats	19%	19%	19%	25%
Weak Democrats	21	20	22	23
Independents	19	21	19	18
Weak Republicans	12	13	13	13
Strong Republicans	13	14	14	11
Never Voted	16	14	11	10
Total	100%	101%	98%	100%
n =	1614	1762	1923	1440

Source: Survey Research Center, University of Michigan.

The advantage the Democrats enjoy nationally is largely a result of the overwhelming majority of Democrats in the South as shown in Table 2.3. If the South is disregarded where there are comparatively few independents and Republicans, the alignment of Democrats and Republicans outside the South is fairly evenly balanced. To an even greater degree *in the North the independents hold the balance of power between Democrats and Republicans.* Furthermore the most one-sided distributions fall in 1964 and reflect an abandonment of the

TABLE 2.3 *The Distribution of Partisans and Independents for the South and Non-South in 1952, 1956, 1960 and 1964.*

	South				Non-South			
	1952	1956	1960	1964	1952	1956	1960	1964
Strong Democrats	24%	24%	22%	33%	17%	17%	18%	22%
Weak Democrats	21	25	29	26	21	18	19	21
Independents	8	12	13	11	24	25	23	22
Weak Republicans	4	6	8	7	15	15	16	16
Strong Republicans	5	6	11	8	17	17	17	12
Never Voted	38	26	18	15	7	8	7	8
Total	100%	99%	101%	100%	101%	100%	100%	101%
n =	433	513	645	443	1140	1247	1278	997

Source: Survey Research Center, University of Michigan.

Republican Party resulting from the Goldwater candidacy. In 1964 the Republicans lost support not only in the North but also in the South where their strategy predicted great gains. It is reasonable to anticipate some fall-off from these atypically pro-Democratic distributions in the years following 1964.

INDEPENDENTS

The independents are the most obvious source of additional votes for either party, given the composition of the national electorate. While loyal supporters of a party sometimes abandon it, as Democrats voted for Eisenhower in large numbers or as Republicans voted for Johnson in preference to Goldwater, year after year the largest bloc of voters available to both parties is the independents. Table 2.2 shows that independents account for about one-fifth of the national electorate and Table 2.4 indicates the independent's capacity for shifting back and forth between the major parties. In recent years each party has successfully appealed to the independents on occasion and won over a large majority to its side.

TABLE 2.4   *The Distribution of Votes for President by Independents from 1940 to 1964.*

	1940	1944	1948	1952	1956	1960	1964
Democratic	61%	62%	57%	33%	27%	46%	66%
Republican	39	38	43	67	73	54	34
Total	100%	100%	100%	100%	100%	100%	100%
n =	?	?	?	263	309	298	219
	(Gallup Poll)			(Survey	Research		Center)

Source: George Gallup. *The Political Almanac,* 1952, p. 38 and Survey Research Center, University of Michigan.

It is appropriate to inquire on what basis the independents switch their party preferences. One of the contentions of the major voting studies has been that the popular view of political independents as intelligent, informed, dispassionate evaluators of candidates, parties and issues is mistaken. Studies from the Bureau of Applied Social Research and the Survey Research Center have supported the view that partisans of both parties are better informed and more concerned with politics than the independents. This analysis has been reflected recently in the campaign strategies of both Democratic and Republican organizations. Increasingly the view has become that the available voters, the voters that can be won over to either party, are an uninformed, apathetic group in whom intelligent appeals to issues and reasoned debate would be lost. (Some differences in perspective are involved here. If one is concerned only with the individuals in the electorate who have not made a choice between Presidential candidates, say, by the last two weeks of the campaign, they are indeed an uninformed, apathetic lot and it is difficult to find any basis for their eventual vote choice. If on the other hand one is concerned with all the individuals who are available sometime between one election and the next or who switch preferences between elections, they are not at all uninformed and apathetic in comparison with standpat voters.)[5]

The case against the independents has been overstated. It is true that independents are not as interested in campaigns or as concerned with which candidate wins as partisans, and this rather dramatic

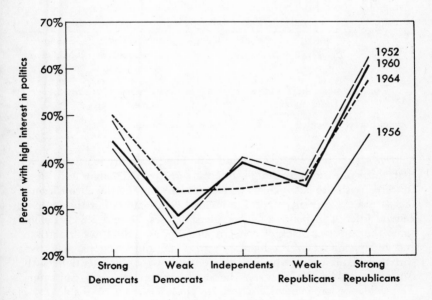

FIGURE 2.8
Interest Among Partisans and Independents in
1952, 1956, 1960 and 1964.

Source: Survey Research Center, University of Michigan.

[5] The most extensive analysis of this point is in V. O. Key, Jr., *The Responsible Electorate* (Cambridge: Belknap Press of Harvard University Press, 1966).

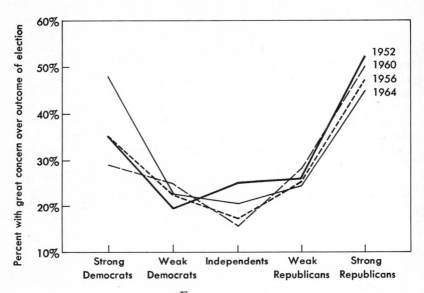

FIGURE 2.9
*Concern with the Outcome of the Election Among Partisans and
Independents in 1952, 1956, 1960 and 1964.*

Source: Survey Research Center, University of Michigan.

pattern is shown in Figures 2.8 and 2.9. The possibility exists, however,
that these measures of "high interest" in the campaign and "great
concern" with the outcome of the election are tapping the enthusiasm of
the partisans for their party's Presidential candidate rather than a more
general interest in politics. Nonetheless Figures 2.8 and 2.9 do demonstrate the consistent lack of concern and interest among weak partisans
and independents in Presidential campaigns and elections. This is a
partial explanation of why it is so difficult to get the attention of the
American public during even the most exciting political campaigns.
The evidence on general interest in politics shown in Table 2.5 is
inconclusive since strong Republicans appear more interested than
others who show similar patterns.

With the other indicators of interest and involvement in politics
a different pattern emerges. In the level of ideological conceptualization,
or seeing parties and candidates in ideological perspective, there are no
differences between partisans and independents. The only difference
is between Republicans and Democrats; Republicans with their higher
level of education are more likely to view politics ideologically. On a

TABLE 2.5   *Distribution of Interest in Government and Politics Generally According to Partisanship, 1964.*

Interested	STRONG DEMOCRAT	WEAK DEMOCRAT	INDEPENDENT	WEAK REPUBLICAN	STRONG REPUBLICAN
All the time	29%	27%	33%	31%	51%
Some of the time	46	40	46	46	34
Only now and then	18	20	12	14	12
Hardly at all	7	12	10	9	3
NA	—	*	—	—	—
Total	100%	99%	101%	100%	100%
n =	366	324	262	187	156

Source: Survey Research Center, University of Michigan.

sense of political efficacy, that is, how significant one views his political activities, the same results obtain: there are no differences between independents and partisans but Republicans have a higher sense of political efficacy than Democrats.

It is surprising that with all the political survey research no satisfactory measure of political information has been developed. It has never been ascertained how well-informed different participants are. It is possible, as a substitute for a measure of political information, to report whether or not individuals have opinions on issues and make the assumption that the individuals who have no opinions are poorly informed. Again using this measure, there are no differences between partisans and independents, so by this test there is no basis for saying independents are less well-informed than partisans, using our definitions of independent and partisan.

The most nearly correct view of the independent, I believe, is that independents are not much interested in politics and government and certainly not much concerned with partisan politics—they are not emotionally involved in party clashes. On the other hand independents appear to have the information and the perspective on political affairs necessary for an evaluation of issues and candidates as competent as could be expected of partisans. Independents are no wiser or more virtuous than partisans; nor are they less so. It is not clear whether their lack of involvement means that independents are not easily aroused by political problems demanding their attention or whether their lack of involvement simply means independents are less biased by partisan predispositions. This uncertainty is troublesome because independents may not be sufficiently motivated to play the role of intelligently mediating disputes between Democrats and Republicans. On the other hand the self-perception of playing this mediating role may motivate independents effectively.

SHIFTING PARTISAN SYMPATHY

Most individuals never alter their partisan loyalties and this stability, in party followers, extends over generations. Very few individuals, less than 2 per cent ordinarily, report a change in party identification in the period of a single year. The net gain or loss to one party in a single year is almost always under 1 per cent. *Since 1936 the shifting of party loyalty has worked to the advantage of the Republicans.* Although some individuals in the electorate are moving away from the Republican Party, more are moving toward it. When we combine this characteristic with the pro-Democratic leanings of new members of the electorate, we find that the Democrats are gradually becoming more numerous and Republicans less numerous. *The advantage Democrats enjoy among new voters more than offsets the losses to the Republicans among older voters.*

It is obviously much easier to change the preferences of voters in particular elections than to alter their basic partisan loyalties. The capacity the electorate has demonstrated to shift support from one party to another is essential if there is to be a believable threat to political office holders. If voting patterns were as stable as partisanship, office holders would be relatively secure once elected. In fact during recent decades Americans have varied their voting patterns greatly while providing the parties with a stable base of underlying loyalty which the parties could usually count on when entering electoral contests. On this score the American electorate appears changeable enough nationally to prevent political leaders from taking the public for granted and stable enough to provide both political parties with an effective base of power from which to threaten the other party.

chapter 3

Social Characteristics
of Partisans and Independents

To this point I have described the voting behavior and political partisanship of Americans without trying to explain these patterns. The major attempts to explain American voting behavior have relied on social and economic factors to account for both the stability and change in American politics. The major studies of the Survey Research Center and the Bureau of Applied Social Research have documented a wide range of relationships in the American electorate between social and economic characteristics and political behavior. Furthermore, social and economic factors form the basis of many descriptions of voting patterns in American journalism and party strategies. Analysis regularly attributes political trends to a "farm revolt" or "fixed income groups" and frequently these explanations rely on so-called bloc voting like "the Negro vote," "the Catholic vote," "the union vote," which imply at least that some social factor causes large numbers of people to vote the same way.

One persistently interesting and convenient way to describe political patterns is by regional distribution of partisans and by the size of the community in which they live. Even casual political commentary tries to distinguish Southern patterns from the rest of the country, and within regions often refers to "the city vote" or "the rural vote." Table 3.1 shows the actual regional and community size composition of strong Democratic and strong Republican partisans for the nation. As we saw above, the Democrats are disproportionately strong in the South, and Southern Democrats account for 40 per cent of all Democrats. The remaining Democrats are fairly evenly spread through the other three

TABLE 3.1   *The Composition of Strongly Partisan Democrats and Republicans According to Region and Community Size in 1964.*

	STRONG DEMOCRATS		STRONG REPUBLICANS	
South	40%		22%	
Cities		9%		6%
Towns		13		11
Rural		18		5
East	19		24	
Cities		12		7
Towns		4		12
Rural		3		5
Midwest	23		37	
Cities		10		8
Towns		7		18
Rural		6		11
Far West	17		16	
Cities		6		7
Towns		7		5
Rural		4		4
Total	99%	99%	99%	99%
n =		363		154

Source: Survey Research Center, University of Michigan.

regions. Within the regions there are some basic differences between Republicans and Democrats. In the South the Democratic strength is in the towns and rural areas while the other major Democratic concentrations are in the cities of the East and Midwest. The Northern Democratic Party is disproportionately urban in contrast to the Southern wing of the party.

The Republican Party on the other hand is disproportionately a small town and medium-sized city party. The main regional bias in the Republican distribution is Midwest strength. In the South, East, and Midwest, Republicans are likely to be in towns: Republicans are also more numerous in Midwestern rural areas. In order not to give the impression that this represents a political description of these areas, it should be pointed out that *Democrats outnumber Republicans in every category* in Table 3.1 *except the towns of the East and Midwest.* These patterns have remained stable in the last several decades except for the general decline in rural population.

POLITICAL AND SOCIAL CHARACTERISTICS

Frequently social descriptions turn to education and family income, occupation of head of household, race and religion. Figure 3.1 examines partisans and independents in 1952 and 1964 on all of these dimensions. The social characteristics of partisans and independents in Figure 3.1 show that in most ways independents look like Republicans. Their levels of education and income are very similar, and the proportions of individuals from professional and managerial households are almost identical among Republicans and independents. The proportion from manual workers' households among independents is closer to the proportion among Democrats. Independents are high in both these occupational categories because they have very low proportions among farmers and retired members of the electorate. It should be obvious from Figure 3.1 that Democrats are much more likely than Republicans to come from manual laborers' households and much less likely to come from white collar households.

Democrats and independents are disproportionately Catholic although there are not great differences in the religious composition of the various political categories. The differences in racial composition are somewhat greater with about one-fifth of the strong Democrats being Negro, while only 1 per cent of the strong Republicans are Negroes. The majority of strong Democrats have not graduated from high school but there are increasingly higher levels of education among each of the other categories as one moves toward the strong Republicans. Farmers are a very small proportion of each category, although the political strength of rural areas is based on more than farm households since many individuals who do not farm live in the country and small towns.

The main conclusion to draw from the Figure 3.1 is that *on most social characteristics Democrats, Republicans and independents are very heterogeneous.* On most characteristics there are substantial proportions all along the political dimension representing a mixed social composition. There are poor Republicans and wealthy Democrats. There are urban Republicans and small town Democrats; manual laborers are Republicans; doctors and lawyers are Democrats. There are Catholic Republicans, Southern Republicans, poorly educated Republicans, and a few Negro Republicans, just as there are well educated Democrats, Midwestern Democrats, and Protestant Democrats. In all cases the tendency runs the other way, but these tendencies and their importance should not be exaggerated.

Socially mixed political groups mean that successful political appeals have been made in the past across social divisions and that social opportunities exist for future political appeals and growth in areas of

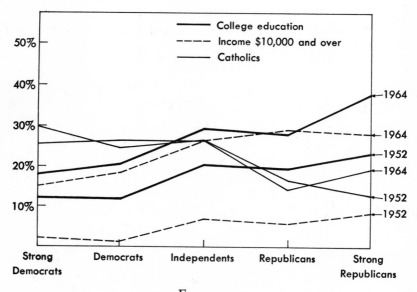

FIGURE 3.1
Social Characteristics of Partisans and Independents in 1952 and 1964.
Source: Survey Research Center, University of Michigan.

current weakness. Socially mixed political groups are evidence of many years of political pluralism, of years of relatively non-doctrinaire political parties appealing to voters where they could find them.

Many of the social groupings which appear quite Democratic in 1964 have also had periods of Republican loyalty. Some Catholics, particularly Italian Catholics, Negroes, some Jewish groups, to mention only a few current Democratic strongholds, have been Republican in earlier periods. These old loyalties die hard and provide a basis for continuing to appeal to these groups. Another source of political variation in social groups is the possibility of a group being Democratic in one community and Republican in another. Adding together these local differences creates an overall pattern of political variation.

A slightly more complicated way to investigate the distribution of partisans and independents is shown in Table 3.2. By controlling for certain characteristics, starting with region and race, and where group size permits controlling in addition on religion and occupation, the partisan distributions of fourteen groupings are presented for 1964. There is a clear Democratic advantage in most groupings. The well-known Democratic dominance in the South appears in the distributions of Negroes and all occupational categories among whites. Neither the upper nor lower socio-economic have deviated from the basic Southern pattern of Democratic loyalty, although the white collar grouping is noticeably less strong as Democratic partisans and the retired are slightly more Republican. In the North what might be called the "minority groups," the Negroes, Jews and Catholics, are heavily pro-Democratic. The manual workers among both Catholics and Protestants are pro-Democratic although Catholic manual laborers are considerably more Democratic than the Protestant manual laborers. Retired Catholics and blue collar Catholics reveal strong pro-Democratic loyalties while the Jewish grouping and the white collar Catholics are less likely to be strongly partisan and more likely to be independents. The Republicans enjoy an advantage in partisan loyalty in only two groupings, the white collar category and the retired category among Northern white Protestants. Independents are numerous in several groupings, particularly among Jews and white collar Catholics, but they are scattered throughout the groupings except in the South. There is no particular social haven of independents.

Several distinctive political patterns in the American electorate are partially revealed by these configurations of data. The retired Catholics and retired Protestants are more strongly partisan than other Catholics and Protestants, and this is a reflection of the overall tendency in the electorate for the older members of society to be more partisan and younger individuals to be more independent. The strength of identification with a party increases the more years one holds the identification. Also Table 3.2 shows that individuals in farm households

TABLE 3.2   *Partisanship Groupings in 1964 According to Region, Race, Religion, and Occupation.*[a]

	SOUTH White				Negro		NON-SOUTH White							
							Jewish	Catholic			Protestant			
	White collar	Blue collar	Farmer	Re-tired	Negro	Negro		White collar	Blue collar	Re-tired	White collar	Blue collar	Farmer	Re-tired
	%	%	%	%	%	%	%	%	%	%	%	%	%	%
Strong Democrat	24	35	40	41	40	56	28	18	31	45	15	16	10	14
Democrat	33	25	23	25	17	10	22	30	27	16	15	25	35	12
Independent	19	9	10	4	6	12	42	28	21	16	20	21	13	15
Republican	8	5	7	13	1	10	8	8	7	13	22	17	23	24
Strong Republican	10	7	10	13	—	2	—	12	4	6	21	9	13	32
Apolitical, non-voter	6	18	10	5	36	10	—	4	10	3	6	13	6	3
Total	100	99	100	100	100	100	100	100	100	99	99	101	100	100
n =	143	199	30	56	89	59	36	110	116	31	201	223	31	78

Source: Survey Research Center, University of Michigan.

[a] These categories account for 83% of the electorate in 1964 and no category which accounts for more than 2% is excluded from the table.

are more likely to be weak partisans regardless of which party they support. This is a reflection of the tendency of farmers to be extremely unstable in their voting patterns and to shift their partisan support more easily and more often than other members of the electorate. Their weaker commitment to the parties facilitates swings in voting and leads to greater variation in turnout. Some observers argue that these traits of farmers increase their political power because candidates appeal to them disproportionately on the chance that they may benefit from the farmers' capacity to shift large numbers of votes.

During the twelve years for which there is appropriate national survey data the distributions within these groupings are remarkably stable, just as the overall distributions of party identification are stable for the same period. There were two substantial changes. One is the decline of permanent non-voters in the South, which has increased the proportions in all the partisan categories but left Democratic dominance unchanged. The other change is among Northern white Protestants and shown in Figure 3.2, where it can be seen that from 1952 to 1964 Republican strength increased among farmers and the retired while Republican strength declined among white collar and blue collar workers.

FIGURE 3.2
Changing Partisanship of Non-Southern White Protestants from 1952 to 1964 According to Occupation.

Source: Survey Research Center, University of Michigan.

SOCIAL COMPOSITION OF
POLITICAL GROUPINGS

There are advantages in looking at essentially the same data in a different way, since it is also possible to examine the social characteristics of political categories. To simplify the analysis Table 3.3 shows

TABLE 3.3 *The Composition of Strong Partisans and Independents in 1964 According to Region, Race, Religion and Occupation.*

| | SOUTH | | |
	Strong Democrats	Independents	Strong Republicans
White			
White collar	24%	57%	40%
Blue collar	24	19	20
Farmer	8	6	9
Retired	16	4	20
Negro	24	11	—
NA (on one or more items)	4	2	11
Total	100%	99%	100%
n =	148	47	35
	NON-SOUTH		
White			
Protestant			
White collar	14%	19%	36%
Blue collar	16	21	16
Farmer	1	2	3
Retired	5	6	21
Catholic			
White collar	9	14	11
Blue collar	17	11	4
Retired	6	2	2
Jewish	5	7	—
Negro	15	3	1
NA (on one or more items)	11	14	7
Total	99%	99%	101%
n =	218	215	121

Source: Survey Research Center, University of Michigan.

only strong Democrats, independents, and strong Republicans. This form of analysis shows what the partisans and independents are like socially in the South and in the non-South. This presentation helps to avoid drawing incorrect conclusions about the composition of our political groupings. For example, even though Jews in the North are strongly pro-Democratic, they are so few in number that they account for only 5 per cent of all Democrats. White collar Protestants in the North are unlikely to be Democrats, but they are so numerous generally that they rank among the largest categories.

Several basic points should be made about the political groupings. First, in the North and the South Democrats are more diverse socially than Republicans with white collar and blue collar households contributing substantially to their ranks as well as a sizable bloc of Negroes. In the South the independents are mainly white collar whites with a noticeable minority of blue collar workers, and while Southern Republicans are similar socially they are not so dependent on white collar workers and more dependent on retired people who are frequently migrants. Outside the South a remarkably similar picture emerges, with the Democrats composed of several different social groups, in contrast to the Republicans who are again disproportionately from white collar households. Northern Republicans also have a concentration of retired white Protestants. Northern independents are not unlike Northern Democrats in social composition except that very few independents are Negroes.

Table 3.3 not only shows how effective the political parties have been in appealing to various social groups, it also shows that both parties depend on a range of social groupings for their electoral strength. To put this differently the political parties have the stable loyalties of socially diverse groups and have a strong incentive to retain these faithful supporters by continuing to appeal to them since it is easier to maintain partisanship than to win converts. This incentive in both major political parties deters a political stand that would drastically realign the parties socially.

SOCIAL GROUP ANALYSIS

Social analysis of political behavior has depended mainly on three units: primary groups, secondary groups, and social classes. Briefly these terms have the following meanings: primary groups are the face-to-face groups one associates with, like family, friends, and fellow workers; secondary groups are organizations or collections of individuals with whom one identifies or is identified but are too large to meet with personally; social classes are broad groupings of social positions in society according to status. These are not particularly abstract analytic concepts and their explanatory power depends on common social experiences and circumstances.

PRIMARY GROUPS

The impact of social groups on individual behavior is so commonplace that it needs little elaboration, and the forms of group influence are too varied to discuss them all. First, primary groups will be considered. Although investigations of the political behavior of primary groups are not numerous, *all available evidence indicates that families and groups of friends are very likely to be politically homogeneous.* Groups of workers appear somewhat more mixed politically. Presumably the social forces in families and friendship groups are more intense and more likely to be based on or to result in political unanimity, but in most work situations people are thrown together without an opportunity to self-select themselves into groups by common political values or on any other basis. At least friendship groups, even casual ones, may be formed in such ways that individuals with much in common—including political views—naturally come together.

Table 3.4 reproduces a set of findings originally presented by Campbell, Converse, Miller and Stokes in *The American Voter* from their 1952 national survey. These data on the voter's primary groups do not reflect the indecisiveness of some voters or the extent to which primary groups have mixed preferences or the voting preferences are unknown. Nevertheless, where an individual is aware of a partisan preference, that preference is extremely likely to correspond with his own.

We have avoided the word "conformity" to describe this pattern of primary group behavior because these group processes are more casual and more a matter of give-and-take than "conformity" implies. Most people care very little about politics and it plays a small part in their personal relations. In very few primary groups is politics of any consequence, so the things which happen in the group that lead to political homogeneity are of low salience. One gradually creates and revises an image of the world and evaluations of that image through social pressures, and many of these processes are face-to-face exchanges of information or reassurances that someone else shares views or considers them plausible, realistic, acceptable. Most individuals are not "pressured" by primary groups to conform or to change politically, at least not nearly so much as they influence one another casually by expressing the same ideas and values without even thinking about it. Ordinarily primary groups do not tolerate high levels of political tension and conflict. Also very few people are subject to the social forces of only one or two primary groups, so "conformity" to group pressure would mean "conformity" to a large number of groups.

In addition to what happens within primary groups there is another factor that produces political similarity and that is the likelihood that primary group members share the same social background and experiences outside the group. *It is most probable that members of any primary group are socially, economically, ethnically, racially alike, and being alike in these ways means that the same general social influences are at work on them.* Much happens outside the primary group to make it politically homogeneous.

TABLE 3.4 *Relation of Reported Partisan Preference of Primary Groups to Respondent's Own Partisan Choice, 1952.*[a]

RESPONDENT VOTED	SPOUSE VOTED		FAMILY VOTED[b]		FRIENDS VOTED		WORK ASSOCIATES VOTED	
	Dem.	Rep.	Dem.	Rep.	Dem.	Rep.	Dem.	Rep.
Democratic	89%	7%	80%	8%	83%	15%	79%	24%
Republican	11	93	20	92	17	85	21	76
Total	100%	100%	100%	100%	100%	100%	100%	100%
n[c] =	337	496	75	108	355	574	271	290

[a] This tabulation is limited to persons who reported voting for a major-party candidate for President and who could attribute to the primary group in question a clear partisan preference.

[b] Asked only of unmarried respondents.

[c] Includes a small number of persons who voted for a minor-party candidate.

Source: Angus Campbell *et al.*, *The American Voter* (New York: Wiley, 1960), p. 77, Table 4.3.

SECONDARY GROUPS

"Secondary groups" refers to the level of social organization between primary groups and social classes. This covers a range of groups and groupings in society like labor unions, religious organizations, and occupational groupings. *Secondary groups are presumably composed of networks of overlapping primary groups where pressures toward political homogeneity spill over and tend to make the members of secondary groups alike.* In addition the members of secondary groups are likely to be subject to the same social forces outside the group. For example, members of a labor union are likely to be in the same income group, live in the same type of neighborhood, and have the same social and educational background, all of which would tend to make them alike politically.

A third factor at work is the role a secondary group may play as a reference group. A group serves as a reference group for an individual if he uses the group as a guide in forming opinions. For example, if a union member identifies with his labor union and he perceives that a particular policy is good for his union and if he favors the policy because of the perceived advantage to his union, then the union is a political reference group for the individual. In the same way if a union member believes that other union members support a policy and if he supports the policy in part for this reason, the union members serve as a reference group. Also, if a white collar worker perceives that unions favor a policy and he opposes it in part for that reason, the union serves as a negative reference group for him.

The most sophisticated analysis of social groups and political behavior applied to national survey data appears in *The American Voter*.[1] The authors demonstrated a distinctive influence on political behavior attributed to secondary group membership among union members, Negroes, Catholics and Jews by controlling on many outside social influences with matched groups. They were able to show that these groups except for Catholics were considerably more Democratic than one would expect from the group members' other social characteristics, such as urban-rural residence, region and occupation status. These findings from *The American Voter* are shown in Table 3.5, and the positive figures represent the additional pro-Democratic influence on individuals supplied by particular group memberships.

Even greater influence is present if the individual identifies with the group. In order to establish the importance of identification with the group and belief in the legitimacy of the group's involvement in politics, the distributions of union members, Negroes, Catholics and Jews in Table 3.6 were presented in *The American Voter*. The increasing impact of identification and perceived legitimacy is demonstrated by the increasing magnitude of the Democratic percentages moving from the lower right-hand corner of Table 3.6 up and to the left. *The stronger the belief in legitimacy and the stronger the group identification, the greater the impact of group standards.*

For all that, in American society large secondary groups are politically heterogeneous. Apparently even these pro-Democratic secondary groups are made up of dissimilar primary groups; to some extent the members are subject to dissimilar social forces. Possibly the significance of secondary groups would appear greater if they were

---

[1] Angus Campbell *et al.*, *The American Voter*, pp. 295–332.

TABLE 3.5   *Distinctiveness of Presidential Vote among Certain Groups, with Life Situation Controlled, 1956.*[a]

	1956 PRESIDENTIAL VOTE
Members of union households	+17.1
Union members	+20.4
Catholics	+ 2.9
Negroes	
Non-South	+11.6
South	+15.4
Jews	+45.4

[a] The entry in each cell represents a deviation in per cent Democratic of the two-party vote within the test group from a comparable per cent computed for control groups matched with the test groups for a variety of conditions of life situation.

Source: Angus Campbell *et al., The American Voter* (New York: Wiley, 1960), p. 306, Table 12.2.

TABLE 3.6   *Presidential Vote Across Four Secondary Membership Groups with Democratic Voting Standards, by Strength of Group Identification and Belief in Legitimacy of Group Political Activity, 1956.*[a] *(Survey Research Center, University of Michigan).*

Belief in Legitimacy of Group Political Activity	GROUP IDENTIFICATION			
	High	Medium	Low	Total
Strong	72%	64%	55%	65%
Medium	62%	55%	45%	53%
Weak	67%	45%	33%	41%
Total	69%	56%	43%	

[a] Each cell entry represents the per cent Democratic of the two-party vote for the appropriate combination of group identification and sense of legitimacy. The "Total" column shows the simple relationship between legitimacy and the vote, with no control on identification. The "Total" row shows the simple relationship between identification and the vote, without control on legitimacy.

Source: Angus Campbell *et al., The American Voter* (New York: Wiley, 1960), p. 322, Table 12.8.

investigated in a narrower, more limited way, rather than aggregated nationally. Essentially this is what the original community voting studies from the Bureau of Applied Research at Columbia University did in Erie County and Elmira.[2] They looked at secondary groups in a single community and found these group memberships explained a large part of the observed political opinions and voting behavior. Certainly many politicians operate as if local secondary groups were politically homogeneous, and national data cannot dismiss this possibility.

RELIGION AND VOTING BEHAVIOR

Usually the voting patterns of American religious groups are not particularly distinctive or at least other factors are considered more important in determining vote choice. The 1960 Presidential election provides a good example of how secondary groups become relevant in a particular election and temporarily have great influence on voting behavior. Kennedy's Catholicism was a major issue throughout the campaign and of great salience to both Catholics and non-Catholics.

The Survey Research Center researchers separated Protestant Democrats according to the frequency with which they attend church and compared each group's defection from Kennedy by calculating the normal defection of the group. Figure 3.3 shows their findings. In both the South and North those who are more regular in church attendance are more likely to defect from the Catholic candidate. Among the nominal Protestants who never attend church Kennedy's Catholicism had no such impact.

Although the evidence is meager on this point, political analysts believe that the temporary salience of the religious issue in 1960 and the sharper drawing of social lines around religious boundaries is typical of what happens to many social factors occasionally. *A social factor like religion or union membership or Italian ancestry or wheat farming will become important temporarily during a political campaign after years of low salience, and become unimportant subsequently.* This irregular rising and falling of issues dramatizing social groups is another partial explanation for the political heterogeneity of American social groups. If the issues that dramatize a given social group were constantly salient, there would eventually be a pure partisan realignment of the group. But if the group is politically salient for only one campaign or

[2] The serious student of political behavior must consider these studies, but we will slight them in this introduction because it has proved difficult to translate their findings directly into national patterns. The 1940 study of Erie County is reported in Paul Lazarsfeld, Bernard Berelson and Hazel Gaudet, *The People's Choice,* and the 1948 Elmira study is reported in Bernard Berelson, Paul Lazarsfeld and William McPhee, *Voting.*

FIGURE 3.3
*Defection to Nixon among Protestant Democrats as a
Function of Church Attendance.*[a] *(Survey Research
Center, University of Michigan.)*

[a] The number of Protestant Democrats who "never" attend church in the
South is too small for inclusion.

Source: Angus Campbell *et al., Elections and the Political Order* (New York:
Wiley, 1966) p. 89, Figure 5.1.

so, such major realignment does not occur. Presumably as such issues
are raised there is a slight partisan realignment, but the changing
sailence of groups leads to political heterogeneity rather than pure
divisions.

SOCIAL CLASSES

The third major unit of analysis is social class. Some of the leading
hypotheses of social and political theory link social classes and political
behavior. Generally the expectations surrounding social class include:

1) the social differences in economic and social interests, and 2) these conflicting interests that follow social class lines will be translated into political forces. The critical variable in this view appears to be the salience of social class interests, and *in American society the importance of social class fluctuates but never becomes extremely high.* The major political and sociological theories of social class have taken for granted the supreme importance of class interests but this assumption seems unrealistic in American society. About one-third of all American adults say they never think of themselves as members of a social class.

A majority of Americans are able to place themselves in a general social position if given a choice between "middle class" and "working class" and even "upper" or "lower" within a class. Even though the individual self-ratings are not perfectly congruent with the positions that social analysts would assign them on the basis of characteristics like occupation, income, and education, a general social class structure does exist. The political significance of social class has been shown to

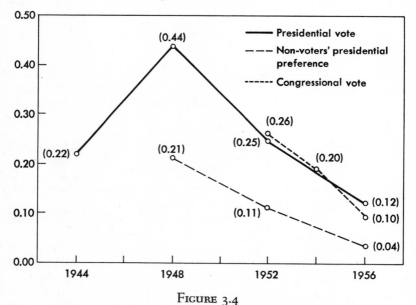

FIGURE 3.4

Status Polarization of Presidential and Congressional Votes, 1944–1956. (Survey Research Center, University of Michigan for the 1948, 1952, and 1956 data; National Opinion Research Center for the 1944 data.)

The points shown represent degree of relationship measured by tau-beta between the occupation status of non-farm respondents and their partisan vote or preference.

Source: Angus Campbell *et al.*, *The American Voter* (New York: John Wiley and Sons, 1960) p. 347, Figure 3.2.

vary by the authors of *The American Voter* in much the same way as for secondary groups. Figure 3.4 from *The American Voter* shows the correlations which indicate the strength of the relationship between social class and vote choice in four elections. The correlations in parentheses mean that in the 1948 Presidential election there was a much stronger relationship between vote choice and social class than in the elections immediately before and after. It is not permissible to infer that social class necessarily caused vote choices in these elections but simply that in 1948 unusually large proportions of middle-class voters supported Dewey, the Republican candidate, and unusually large proportions of working-class voters supported Truman. Or, to describe the pattern a different way, in 1944, 1952 and 1956 there were not substantial differences in the support for Roosevelt and Eisenhower among middle-class and working-class voters. These same patterns of low relationship continue through 1960 and 1964.

With 1964 data we can examine the relationship between social class identification and partisanship. Table 3.7 shows the distribution of partisans in the South and non-South according to four categories of social and class identification. As is so often the case no particular relationship exists in the South since all categories are strongly Democratic. Outside the South the pattern is more striking. Clearly the middle-class identifiers are about equally likely to be Republicans or Democrats while the working-class identifiers are much more likely to be Democrats. Independents are represented throughout in about the same proportions although further analysis reveals that disproportionately large numbers of independents are weak identifiers with the working class who have blue collar occupations or weak identifiers with the working class who have high status white collar occupations.

It is to be expected that partisanship would be more highly correlated with voting than is social class identification, but there is the possibility that social class will be strongly related to opinions on political issues and particularly on those issues where real class differences might be expected. Table 3.8 shows the distribution of opinion on two such issues, Medicare and federal aid to education, for social class categories. There are indeed differences in opinions associated with social class identification and in the expected direction—the working-class respondents are more in favor of Medicare and federal aid to education and middle-class respondents more opposed.

However, these relationships can be accounted for by the presence of differing numbers of partisans in the social class categories. Or, to put it differently, middle-class respondents appear more conservative on Medicare and federal aid to education because more Republicans are in the middle-class categories and Republicans are conservative on these issues. Working-class individuals appear more liberal because there are proportionally more liberal Democrats in the working class.

TABLE 3.7 *Distribution of Partisanship According to Social Class Identification and Region in 1964.*

| | SOUTH | | | |
| | Middle Class | | Working Class | |
	Feel close	Do not feel close	Feel close	Do not feel close
Strong Democrat	38%	33%	27%	36%
Democrat	23	16	30	28
Independent	15	13	7	7
Republican	9	13	4	6
Strong Republican	8	16	5	5
Apolitical, non-voter	8	10	28	18
Total	101%	101%	101%	100%
n =	104	63	101	158

| | NON-SOUTH | | | |
| | Middle Class | | Working Class | |
	Feel close	Do not feel close	Feel close	Do not feel close
Strong Democrat	19%	12%	22%	33%
Democrat	20	22	22	23
Independent	19	23	24	19
Republican	19	21	15	9
Strong Republican	21	14	7	6
Apolitical, non-voter	2	8	10	9
Total	100%	100%	100%	99%
n =	215	181	248	288

Source: Survey Research Center, University of Michigan.

Furthermore middle-class Democrats are just as liberal as working-class Democrats and working-class Republicans are about as conservative as middle-class Republicans. Actually *there is some variation associated with social class that is independent of partisanship but the relationship with partisanship and these issues is about three times as strong as the relationship between social class and the issues.* Social class may serve as a political guide for some citizens on certain issues but it does not appear to be extremely important in American politics. As much as anything else this is a reflection of the tendency of political leaders not to emphasize highly divisive social class issues.

Next to Canada the United States is usually regarded as an extreme case among developed democracies for the insignificance of social class

TABLE 3.8 *Distribution of Attitudes Toward Federal Aid to Education and Medical Care for the Aged According to Social Class Identification for the Non-South in 1964.*

	MIDDLE CLASS		WORKING CLASS	
	Feel Close	Do not Feel Close	Feel Close	Do not Feel Close
Favors Medicare	40%	33%	46%	54%
Favors but has doubts	2	3	9	7
Depends, other	7	9	5	7
Opposes but has doubts	6	5	2	2
Opposes Medicare	35	37	22	15
Don't know, no interest	10	13	17	16
Total	100%	100%	101%	101%
Favors federal aid	22%	20%	25%	29%
Favors but has doubts	3	3	6	6
Depends, other	9	8	4	5
Opposes but has doubts	11	10	7	9
Opposes federal aid	44	43	36	31
Don't know, no interest	11	16	23	20
Total	100%	100%	101%	101%
n =	209	166	222	261

Source: Survey Research Center, University of Michigan.

for political behavior; in most European democracies social class is of greater consequence.[3] Two factors may depress the apparent relationship between social class and voting behavior in the United States. Aggregating data for the entire population may cover up stronger relationships for sub-groups and in particular communities. Furthermore, American political leaders make broad appeals intended to cross and disrupt social class lines. One interpretation of American political history portrays the twentieth century in terms of suppressing class issues and making politics unimportant for and uninteresting to the lower social classes.[4]

[3] There are several important works on social class and political behavior in addition to *The American Voter*, chap. 13. Students interested in this area of analysis should see Robert Alford, *Party and Society* (Chicago: Rand McNally and Company, 1963) and Heinz Eulau, *Class and Party in the Eisenhower Years* (New York: The Free Press, 1962).

[4] The major argument is made by E. E. Schattschneider, *The Semi-Sovereign People.*

SOCIAL CROSS PRESSURES

One of the major concerns of the early voting studies by Lazarsfeld, Berelson and other researchers at the Bureau of Applied Social Research of Columbia University was the "cross pressure hypothesis," and this perspective will be used to examine some short-run and long-run influence on political acts. The cross pressure hypothesis is simple in outline, but it can be confusing because it takes so many different forms. The hypothesis is based on the existence of two (or more) forces or tendencies, one in a Republican direction and the other in a Democratic direction. Sometimes this is stated as two factors *predisposing* a voter in a Republican or a Democratic direction. Usually the hypothesis is presented with two social dimensions like occupation and religion:

Occupation:

     White collar   Blue collar
     ←——————————————→
     Pro-Republican   Pro-Democratic

Religion:

     Protestant   Catholic
     ←——————————————→
     Pro-Republican   Pro-Democratic

Some individuals are *predisposed* or pushed in a consistent way such as white collar Protestants with both occupation and religion predisposing them in a Republican direction or blue collar Catholics predisposed in a Democratic direction.

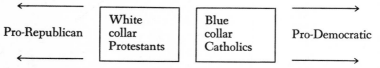

But some individuals are predisposed in both directions or "cross pressured."

The cross pressure hypothesis asserts that the individuals who are under consistent pressure behave differently than individuals under cross pressure. The predictions under the hypothesis are:

CONSISTENT PRESSURE	CROSS PRESSURE
straight ticket voting	split ticket voting
early decision on vote	late decision on vote
high interest in politics	low interest in politics
high levels of information	low levels of information
consistent attitudes	conflicting attitudes

These expectations about voting behavior under cross pressure are actually specific applications of more general patterns investigated by sociologists and psychologists in a variety of ways. The response to cross pressure predicted by the hypothesis are avoidance reactions—efforts to avoid or minimize the anxiety produced by conflict.

CROSS PRESSURE AND POLITICAL THEORY

There is another application associated with the cross pressure thesis in empirical political theory. Many large social groups are expected to be stable politically according to the cross pressure hypothesis, i.e., they are consistently predisposed to be Republican or Democratic by the social forces working on them, and therefore social pressures which consistently predispose voters lead to political stability among both Republicans and Democrats because they have politically consistent social backgrounds.

Between these politically consistent social groups there are cross pressured groups predisposed toward both parties and according to the cross pressure thesis these groups are politically unstable. These cross pressured groups provide the voters who switch from one party to another, and this means that the available voters, the voters to whom the parties must appeal in order to win new voters, are in a social position between Democrats and Republicans. Consequently, the argument goes, these available voters have social and political attitudes somewhere between Republicans and Democrats. Furthermore, the politically unstable social base means that these voters are easily switched from one party to another, so they are sensitive to political forces even though they are not particularly interested in or informed about politics. Were they highly interested, they would be less flexible.

These arguments lead to a reassuring view of the American electorate. There is a widespread political stability based on a relatively stable social system. Political flexibility and sensitivity are provided by groups in between the partisans and therefore politically moderate groups. As long as the stable partisan groups are roughly of the same size, stable competitive conditions are guaranteed. As long as there is some overlapping of social groups, these will be the necessary cross pressures to produce the switching political moderates. It appears to be an electoral system with no weaknesses.

Nevertheless, there are some difficulties with this picture of an electoral system. For one thing *the social cross pressure thesis is merely a tendency and not perfectly descriptive of the impact of social forces on political behavior.* The politically stable are more heterogeneous than the above account implies, and *the politically flexible are not under dramatic social cross pressure according to the best data available.*

Discussion supporting the cross pressure thesis is most extensive in the Elmira study, *Voting* by B. Berelson, P. Lazarsfeld and W. McPhee. Figure 3.5 shows a set of findings from *Voting* reflecting the impact

FIGURE 3.5
Proportion of Voters Making Vote Choice for President in October or Later According to Presence or Absence of Cross Pressures, Elmira, 1948. (Bureau of Applied Social Research, Columbia University.)

Source: B. Berelson, P. Lazarsfeld and Wm. McPhee, *Voting* (Chicago: University of Chicago Press, 1954), p. 131, Chart LXV.

of cross pressure on time of individual decisions on how to vote. There is a very slight tendency for cross pressures caused by religion and socioeconomic status to be associated with late decisions on voting. There are stronger relationships associated with conflicts in primary groups.

There is a stronger cross pressure relationship reported in *The American Voter*, although it predicts a somewhat different pattern behavior from those discussed above. The authors of *The American Voter* postulated that social cross pressures would lead to conflicting political attitudes. Table 3.9 shows the higher level of conflicting political attitudes among white collar Catholics, the group under cross pressure presumably, in comparison with blue collar Catholics for each number of attitudes.

Several other patterns of social variables have been treated as a source of cross pressure. One of these is upward and downward social

TABLE 3.9 *Proportion of Catholics Showing Some Conflict of Partisan Attitude by Occupation and Level of Attitude, 1956. (Survey Research Center, University of Michigan.)*

	Two Partisan Attitudes	Three Partisan Attitudes	Four Partisan Attitudes	Five Partisan Attitudes
Blue Collar	15%	45%	45%	74%
Business or Professional	50%	47%	59%	85%

Source: Angus Campbell *et al., The American Voter* (New York: John Wiley and Sons, 1960), p. 88, Table 4.6.

mobility. To put it simply the argument has been that upwardly mobile individuals abandon a Democratic identification and become Republicans, while the downwardly mobile abandon the Republican Party to become Democrats. During the period of maximum social and political stress associated with this mobility the individual becomes an independent. It would be easier to test this argument if it were easier to measure social mobility. Table 3.10 from *The American Voter* uses

TABLE 3.10 *Relation of Reported Changes in Own Occupational Status to Changes in Self-Identification with Parties, 1956. (Survey Research Center, University of Michigan.)*

	Occupational Mobility	
	Down	Up
Changes in party identification		
From Republican to Democratic	28%	24%
From Republican to Independent	8	12
From Democratic to Independent	32	29
From Democratic to Republican	32	35
Total	100%	100%
n =	47	121

Source: Angus Campbell *et al., The American Voter* (New York: John Wiley and Sons, 1960), p. 459, Table 16.8.

change from first job to present job as a measure of occupational mobility, and the distributions in Table 3.10 do not provide much support for the hypothesis. There is, in fact, very little political difference between the upwardly and downwardly mobile and this appears to hold for several measures of mobility.

Actually the only form of cross pressure that is strongly confirmed by national survey data is attitudinal cross pressure. Attitudes toward the candidates and parties were measured by the Survey Research Center in 1952 and 1956 and conflicting attitudes, i.e., an individual holding pro-Democratic and pro-Republican attitudes, were associated with non-voting, indecision and indifference toward the election. It is still not possible, however, to treat the conflicting attitudes as the cause of these patterns of behavior. It is quite possible that the attitudes and the withdrawal behavior is caused by some third factors.

The American electoral system appears to operate in a way predicted by the cross pressure hypothesis. There is partisan stability among both Republicans and Democrats, and the shifting of political fortunes is accomplished without intensity or extreme political appeals. We should, however, be skeptical of explaining these political patterns as a result of the social forces postulated by the cross pressure thesis. Neither short-run partisan stability nor independent flexibility appears strongly associated with social group predispositions. Two conclusions can be drawn about social characteristics and voting behavior. On the one hand social factors like race, religion and occupation as well as primary groups have been shown to be related to partisanship. *The long-run social and political patterns in the American electorate appear related.* On the other hand the short-run impact of social groups on voting behavior appears uneven and insignificant generally. Occasionally social groups appear important nationally as religion did in 1960 and under certain conditions social cross pressures may operate, but *normally we do not expect social factors to show the same consistent, strong patterns with vote choice that we have found with partisanship.*

chapter 4

Public Opinion and Ideology

VOTING BEHAVIOR IS NOT THE ONLY SIGNIFICANT ASPECT OF AMERICAN political behavior. Several aspects of the study of public opinion are not directly related to voting behavior. One persistent concern of analysts of public opinion is the attitudes of people toward issues of the day. Another concern is political ideology, particularly liberalism-conservatism and internationalism-isolationism, and of increasing interest is consensus or the beliefs of the general public about how the political system should work.

PUBLIC OPINION ON POLITICAL ISSUES

The commercial opinion polling organizations have spent thirty years asking Americans about their views on matters of public policy, and most of this investigation has taken the form of asking individuals whether they "approve or disapprove of," "agree or disagree" with a statement of policy or asking them to pick their preference among two or more alternative statements of policy. This form of questioning seriously exaggerates the number of people who hold views on political issues. It is easy for people to say "agree" or "disapprove" in response to a question even if they know nothing at all about the topic. If given the opportunity many people will volunteer the information that they hold no views on the matters of public policy. Table 4.1 from *The American Voter* shows the proportion of the electorate admitting it has no opinions on major policy questions in 1956. The proportion with no opinion on an issue varies from one-tenth to almost one-third of the electorate and to these proportions may be added as substantially uninformed those individuals who hold an opinion but who do not have any idea what the government is doing in the policy area. Beyond these two categories of relatively uninformed individuals, the work of Philip Con-

TABLE 4.1　*Public Familiarity with Selected Issues, 1956. (Survey Research Center, University of Michigan.)*

Issue	No Opinion	Hold Opinion But Do Not Know What Gov't Is Doing	Hold Opinion Know What Gov't Is Doing	Total
Foreign Policy				
Give aid to neutral countries	28%	19	53	100%
Send soldiers abroad	20%	13	67	100%
Economic aid to foreign countries	17%	16	67	100%
Act tough toward Russia, China	20%	11	69	100%
Avoid foreign involvement	14%	15	71	100%
Friendliness toward other nations	12%	10	78	100%
Domestic Policy				
Firing of suspected Communists	16%	39	45	100%
Leave electricity, housing to private industry	30%	19	51	100%
Segregation of schools	12%	34	54	100%
Influence of big business in government	23%	18	54	100%
Influence of unions in government	25%	20	55	100%
Insure medical care	12%	29	59	100%
Cutting taxes	19%	18	63	100%
Government guarantee of jobs	10%	23	67	100%
Racial equality in jobs and housing	14%	19	67	100%
Government aid to education	10%	23	67	100%

Source: Angus Campbell *et al., The American Voter* (New York: John Wiley and Sons, 1960), p. 174, Table 4-1.

verse shows that among the individuals who appear to have an opinion there are a number who ought to be regarded as responding to policy questions at random.[1]

There are a number of ways of explaining this lack of opinion and information on topics of public policy. Generally the same factors which explain non-voting account for the absence of opinions. *Individuals with little interest in or concern with politics are least likely to have opinions on matters of public policy.* Beyond this basic relationship low socio-economic status is associated with no opinion on issues; *low income and little education create social circumstances in which individuals are less likely to have views and information on public policies.*

FUNCTIONS OF OPINIONS FOR INDIVIDUALS

Most discussions of political opinions imply a more or less reasoned handling of opinions by individuals; that is, that individuals intelligently relate their opinions to one another and that there is a logical relation between goals and preferences for policies leading to goals. While undoubtedly there is much reasoned opinion formation in the American public, not all opinions are mere rational deductions from goals and means to those goals. Social psychology suggests that opinions can serve various purposes for an individual and these functions are cognitive, social and psychological. This consideration raises the possibility that opinions may not be related to political behavior and political opinions may not be related to one another.

To put it very simply, an opinion may serve purposes for an individual that are not dependent on its social, economic or political meaning but rather depend on elements of the opinion having special psychological significance for an individual. For example, an individual might hold opinions strongly prejudicial against some group because it enhances his self-esteem to feel superior to some others, or he might imagine that some group has undesirable qualities of which he rids himself by projecting them onto the group. An individual may view a political situation, say the clash between the United States and China, as analogous to more personal conflict situations to which he attaches considerable emotion. There are no limits to the possible attachments of psychological significance to elements of public opinion, but the importance of these attachments should not be exaggerated. The danger or disadvantage of psychological attachments of this kind is that the opinions are not responsive to ordinary influence because of their psy-

[1] Philip Converse, "The Nature of Belief Systems in Mass Publics," in David Apter, ed., *Ideology and Discontent* (New York: The Free Press of Glencoe, 1964), pp. 238-45.

chological importance to the individual. Either because of widespread personality characteristics or because of the low salience of political issues, *most Americans do not appear to attach strong psychological meaning to their political opinions* or at least not such strong emotional associations that political opinions are highly inflexible. Furthermore *it is unlikely in a modern pluralistic society that an opinion on a significant political subject will remain solely of psychological relevance for an individual; the opinion will also take on social and cognitive functions.*

Opinions serve a social function if they aid the individual in adjusting to others or in becoming part of a group. (In some cases individuals may use opinions to set themselves apart from others.) Political and social issues may be too unimportant generally to serve social purposes for most people, and there is little evidence to indicate that there are strong social conformity pressures on most political issues. Nevertheless for highly salient issues it is likely to be uncomfortable and costly for an individual to hold a socially unacceptable view. Cognitive functions of opinions cover the efforts to give meaning to our social environment and to relate elements of belief and meaning to one another. Generally opinions relate directly or indirectly to an individual's most salient goals or values; somehow the policy supported by a political opinion is expected to be consistent with one's most important political values. This is not necessarily the case and sometimes an individual's opinions are inconsistent.

OPINION CONSISTENCY AND DISSONANCE

The main thrust of scholarly interest in the functions of opinions have been in analysis of opinion change. The general conclusion can be stated simply: *in order to change an opinion its function (or functions) for the individual must be undermined or altered,* or to put it somewhat differently, giving an individual more information or altering the policy implications of an opinion will not necessarily lead to opinion change. The individual may hold his views for the social or psychological purpose it serves, in which case to change the opinion one must undermine or alter the social or psychological purpose served by the views. Nevertheless I would still maintain the perspective on American public opinion which suggests that political opinions are most often changed by simply providing individuals with more information. This additional information may be no more than indications that many political leaders whom an individual respects hold a particular view or some new facts about the environment. The low salience of most political issues plus the widespread emphasis on debate and discussion lead to circumstances which improve the opportunities for changing opinions with information.

The analysis of inconsistency in opinions has much in common with the cross pressure thesis considered in chapter three. This analysis of opinions in psychology has taken the form of identifying elements of several opinions as consistent with one another or as being in conflict (dissonant). Also it is assumed that dissonance is disturbing and an individual will try to avoid or reduce dissonance. Dissonant elements of opinion and information are ideas in conflict. Some examples of dissonance analysis should clarify these concepts. If an individual believes that it is extremely undesirable to use atomic bombs under any circumstances and also believes that the United States must do whatever necessary to halt communism in Southeast Asia, these two opinions are potentially dissonant. Yet an individual might avoid holding strongly dissonant opinions, for example, that the United States should use atomic bombs in Southeast Asia in order to stop communism or that the United States must not take certain steps in opposing communism. Or he may avoid dissonance by holding the view that it would be unwise to use atomic bombs in Southeast Asia since the Communists would turn it to their advantage, or some other opinion that reconciles the potential conflict in the original opinions.

If an individual believes that it is appropriate to treat Negroes as an inferior because he believes they are of inferior intelligence and ability and if he is confronted with new information that Negroes are equal to whites in intelligence and ability, these two elements are in conflict. The dissonance could be reduced by discrediting the source of the new information or rationalizing his attitude toward Negroes on some other basis such as moral or spiritual superiority of whites.

Cognitively consistent patterns are presumably stable, and dissonant patterns are susceptible to change. Furthermore individuals will change dissonant patterns in the easiest way; the opinions or beliefs that are least important to the individual will be changed rather than salient, important ideas or values.

AGGREGATE OPINIONS

It is no simple matter to describe the distributions of opinions in the American electorate because there is no obvious, agreed way in which to measure these opinions. Or to put it another way, by asking different questions in public opinion polls we can get different answers. We could substantially alter distributions of opinions on, say, foreign aid by asking respondents if they approved of "squandering our money abroad" as opposed to "feeding starving children overseas." Furthermore there is no ultimate test of measures of opinions as there is with voting behavior. Consequently descriptions of public opinion must be taken as more subjective, more tentative than the discussion of partisanship because there are no independent indicators of opinions on public issues.

Usually public attitudes on policies in American society are viewed as *permissive opinion*, that is, there is a wide range of government activity acceptable to the public, and ordinarily policy alternatives advocated by the political parties are within the range of permissive agreement. *Negative opinion* exists to the extent there are alternatives which are definitely opposed by the public, and *supportive opinion* exists to the extent that certain policies are demanded. For example, there is undoubtedly widespread supportive opinion for public education in this country; most individuals demand a system of public education or would demand it if it were threatened. At the same time there is permissive support for a wide range of policies and programs in public education. Governments at several levels may engage in a variety of programs without the public becoming aroused to opposition or support. Within this permissive range the public is indifferent. At some point out-and-out opposition to programs in public education develops and negative opinion is formed which imposes a limit on how far government can go. It is no easy matter for political analysts or politicians to discover these boundaries between supportive, permissive and negative opinions, and political leaders deceptively or mistakenly argue that there are supportive opinions for their positions and negative opinions toward their opponents' views. We should be skeptical of these claims because it is much more likely that there are permissive opinions and casual indifference toward the alternative views. Even when individuals express preferences on public policies, these are not likely to be extremely felt and probably represent permissive opinion.

ATTITUDES TOWARD PUBLIC POLICY

There are three common divisions of American opinion on public policy, domestic economic affairs, other domestic affairs, and foreign affairs, in addition to the more general areas of ideology and consensus. The following analysis will investigate each of the areas separately, their interrelationships and the relationship of social characteristics and partisanship with opinions on issues. The leading assumption is that partisan identification provides guidance for the public on policy matters; that is, most Americans hold their opinions by following what they perceive to be the view consistent with their partisanship.

One of the basic beliefs of American politics has been that economic issues are more salient, have more impact on the electorate than other issues. Domestic economic issues are frequently treated by politicians and political analysts as the real forces at work in the political system, sometimes openly and sometimes behind a facade of other issues. There is a certain plausibility to this view and obviously there have been periods when economic issues were paramount, but there is no reason to assume that any one type of issue will always be more important than others. Doubtless there is variation in the salience of issues with economic issues frequently the most prominent and occasionally displaced by foreign policy issues or non-economic domestic issues. In any case in recent years it appears that for some members of the electorate issues like school integration or a Catholic in the White House or escalation of the war in Viet Nam have been of far greater concern than economic issues.

It is not easy to establish the relative salience of domestic affairs and foreign affairs and the measures of salience are quite crude. V. O. Key reports in *Public Opinion and American Democracy*[2] that in discussing the merits and demerits of the parties and candidates in 1952 and 1956 Americans gave domestic matters greater salience than foreign affairs. The breakdown he gives is as follows:

	1952	1956
Foreign affairs more salient	16%	17%
Domestic affairs more salient	47	54
About equal attention to each	8	10
No issue content	29	19

V. O. Key also reports that there was a clear relationship between issue salience and voting with those who gave greater or equal salience to foreign affairs voting for Eisenhower disproportionately. This is merely descriptive of what has happened in recent elections and according to only one form of measurement, i.e., it is simply one way of describing an extremely complex set of factors and interrelationships. It is not a prediction of future voting behavior or a statement of constraints operating in the American electoral system. *The prominence of economic issues should not be taken for granted.*

DOMESTIC ECONOMIC ISSUES

In economic matters Americans are more liberal than conservative. The overall configuration of preferences on public policy in the American electorate can be described as "liberal" in that there is usually a willingness to support federal governmental programs intended to solve social problems. There is no widespread, consistent public opposition to increased government activity in domestic economic affairs and in welfare

[2] V. O. Key, Jr., *Public Opinion and American Democracy*, p. 173.

programs. In recent years the main source of opposition to federal government activities appears to be based on opposition to racial integration and not based on economic considerations. To be sure there are individuals in the electorate who oppose government economic activities for other reasons, but the ideological opponents of government activity are not numerous in the general public. In this respect, as in many others, the public does not reflect the characteristics of the political leaders among whom there are many opponents of "liberal" domestic economic programs. In this respect political leaders are much more conservative than the public.

Figure 4.1 shows some distributions of political attitudes taken

FIGURE 4.1
The Support for Federal Aid to Education and Medical Care for the Aged from 1956 to 1964.

Source: Survey Research Center, University of Michigan.

from Survey Research Center national samples. Only the 1956 and 1960 questions are perfectly comparable so it is not possible to assess changes in public opinion from 1956 to 1964 with these data. There is considerable stability in the aggregate level of support for federal aid to education and medical care programs over the eight-year period. Generally over 50 per cent of the electorate favors these programs with about one-quarter of the population in opposition and the remainder holding qualified views. It is certainly reasonable to expect that views on such issues would be strongly influenced by an individual's social and economic characteristics and Figure 4.2 shows the level of support for medical care in various social groupings. The highest level of support is found among Negroes and Jews, traditionally liberal groups, and while these groups are similar politically, they are extremely dissimilar socially and economically. The Negroes, a low income group, could be expected to need government assistance to secure medical care and immediate self-interest could explain their support as it could explain the support of retired people. But the Jews are a white collar, high income group and most unlikely to hold these views for reasons of self-interest. The Jewish group more than any of those considered here represent the impact of ideology and social doctrine on political opinions. In the other groups there is a gradual increase of support as we move from the white collar occupation through manual laborers to the farmers and retired.

It should be noted that partisans have quite different views on medical care. Figure 4.3 shows that Democratic partisans support medical care strongly—they are more favorable in the North than in the South—and Republican partisans oppose medical care to about the same degree. Partisanship may not lead individuals to hold the views they do, but the stability of an individual's partisanship makes it likely that his views on policy are influenced by his partisanship. Individuals abandon their party over an issue presumably only when they feel exceptionally intensely about the issue. It should be noted that there are extreme or intense differences on very few issues among social groups or among partisans. Seemingly neither social circumstances nor political parties provide such unambiguously persuasive cues for most individuals that their own values and misperceptions cannot operate independently. Political, social and personal factors all diminish the dramatic differences that might exist on public issues.

CIVIL RIGHTS AND INTEGRATION

The main topics of domestic public policy on non-economic matters since World War II have dealt with civil liberties and racial integration issues. In the early 1950's a cluster of issues and problems loosely covered by the term "McCarthyism" was raised over the rights and treatment of individuals accused of treason, socialistic attitudes and various other acts and beliefs. The general public was never as concerned with McCarthyism as the politically attentive were. In the electorate, concern with McCarthyism—either pro or con—never became an element of significant division among social or political groups.

The most persistently volatile issues in American history have

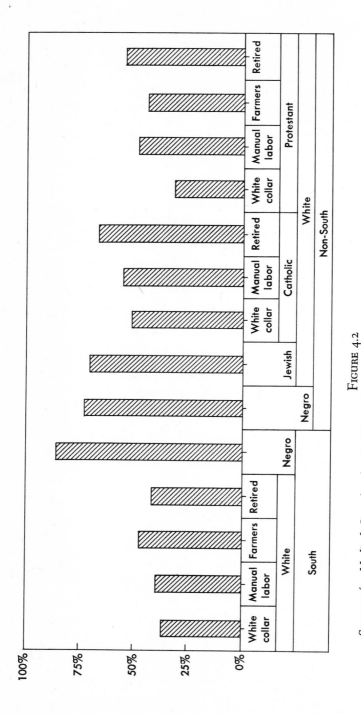

FIGURE 4.2

Support for Medical Care for the Aged in 1964 According to Region, Race, Religion and Occupation.

Source: Survey Research Center, University of Michigan.

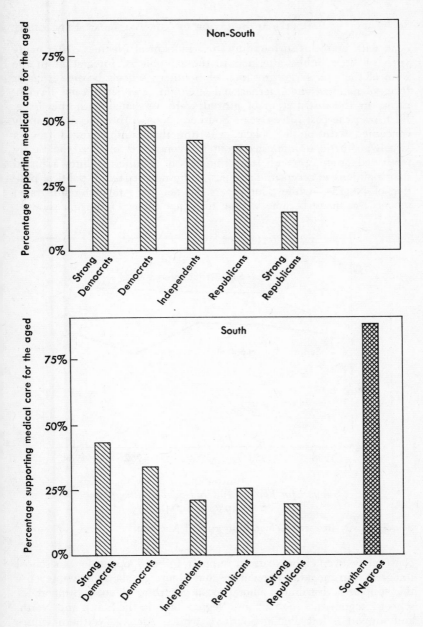

FIGURE 4.3
Support for Medical Care for the Aged in 1964 According to Region and Partisanship.

Source: Survey Research Center, University of Michigan.

dealt with problems surrounding the treatment of Negroes. After many years of little public attention to these problems, integration in the form of the courts' desegregation of Southern schools became a major focus of national and international attention. Two significant developments in the distribution of attitudes are associated with this issue. First, over the past fifteen years Southern Negroes became increasingly concerned with public policies affecting them and changed from a largely apathetic, uninterested group to a concerned, involved, politically motivated group. Second, large numbers of Southern whites adjusted their opinions to accept the realities of the new legal and political position of Negroes—white Southerners did not come to prefer integrated schools but many became willing to accept them. Figure 4.4 shows a

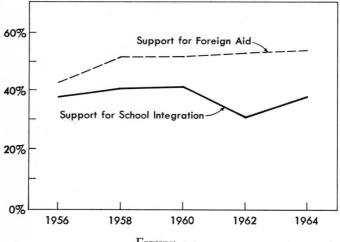

FIGURE 4.4
*Support for Foreign Aid and School Integration
from 1956 to 1964.*

Source: Survey Research Center, University of Michigan.

consistency over eight years in support for and opposition to school integration in the adult population, and Figure 4.5 shows how unevenly this support is distributed among social groups as of 1964. Support for school integration is high among Negroes both in the South and North, and support is low among Southern whites. Among Northern whites the more dramatic differences are associated with religious preference while relatively minor variation is associated with occupational groupings except for farmers who display consistently lower levels of support for integrated schools.

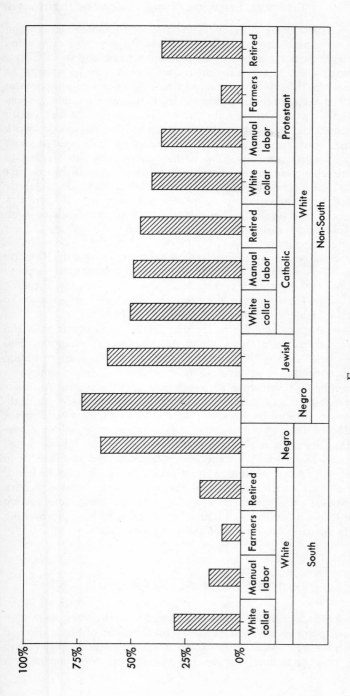

FIGURE 4.5

Support for School Integration According to Region, Race, Religion, and Occupation in 1964.

Source: Survey Research Center, University of Michigan.

In 1964 there were differences in support for school integration associated with partisanship, although when Negroes are eliminated from the distributions the differences among partisans shown in Figure 4.6 are not as great as the differences found among social groups. In the North even though Democrat partisans support integration most frequently and Republican partisans least frequently among independents and weak partisans, the pattern is uneven. In the South among whites, the greatest support for integration is among weak Republicans who are not numerous and least support among weak Democrats who are numerous. On the integration issue, in contrast to the domestic economic issues, the distributions of partisanship do not explain the differences. Probably issues like integration are regularly more related to social groups than to political categories. In part this may be because the leaders of both parties take similar stands on such issues in a given constituency and consequently the parties do not provide differing cues or leadership. In other cases the leaders of one party may disagree among themselves on such issues, perhaps because the leaders represent differing constituencies, and consequently a party will not offer consistent cues and leadership on these matters of public policy. In some circumstances these issues have sufficient salience to overcome the influence of partisan political leadership.

Another area of domestic policy that has received attention is the relation of governmental institutions to religious organizations and particularly state support for parochial education and prayers in public schools. As with the other areas of non-economic domestic policy, in part the public is responding to Supreme Court decisions. Attitudes toward parochial school support are heavily influenced by an individual's perceived religious interests. Generally Americans would prefer more mixing of church and state, not less. For example, about three-fourths of adults support the practice of starting public school classes with a prayer. But to date this preference has not been mobilized into an intense preference or into a political force of any consequence nationally. Issues which might have become volatile politically have been suppressed by the leaders of major religious institutions among others, but the area remains as a temptation to political leaders searching for subjects on which to take potentially popular stands.

FOREIGN AFFAIRS

Like non-economic domestic problems, foreign affairs vary greatly in salience and particularly in response to involvement of the nation in military conflicts. In recent years the main issues of foreign policy have been concern over military policies during conflicts and concern over

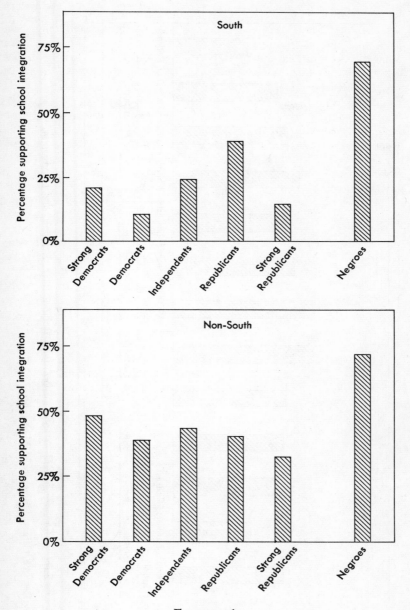

FIGURE 4.6
Support for School Integration in 1964 According to Race, Region and Partisanship.

Source: Survey Research Center, University of Michigan.

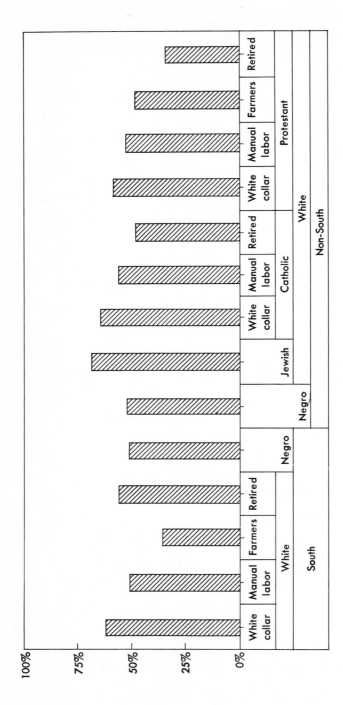

FIGURE 4.7

Support for Foreign Aid in 1964 According to Region, Race, Religion, and Occupation.

Source: Survey Research Center, University of Michigan.

foreign aid at other times. In 1964 the alleged "trigger-happy" approach of Goldwater to international problems became an issue for large numbers of voters and was emphasized by Democrats. Whether justified or not Goldwater's appeal suffered because he was viewed as recklessly belligerent and more likely than his opponent to involve the country in military conflicts.

Opinions on foreign affairs in Figure 4.4 show a high degree of consistency with an absolute majority favoring foreign aid in most years. As Figure 4.7 shows, the differences in support of foreign aid are strongly related to occupational groupings. There do not appear to be important differences in attitudes toward foreign affairs associated with religion or region. These patterns in part reflect the willingness of higher income groups to support programs that imply higher taxes and the unwillingness of lower income groups to do so. This tendency applies to both domestic and foreign policy. Figure 4.8 shows that some relationship in 1964 between partisanship and support of foreign aid exists, but this is largely a function of the greater tendency of Republicans to give qualified support of foreign aid; the opposition to foreign aid is totally unrelated to partisanship and not widespread.

Generally partisanship is strongly related to domestic economic policies and partisan loyalties appear to dominate the attitudes individuals have that might be associated with social and economic groupings independently of political party ties. *Opinions on foreign policy by way of contrast are not related to party identification* and the moderate relationships are with social and economic characteristics. *Attitudes toward various race issues seem related to both partisanship and social variables with the latter the more important.* The sustained investigation of attitudes toward public policies is made difficult by the relatively short time any particular issue is salient and by the changing position of the political parties over the years. In addition a given issue may strike social groups differently over time. With so many elements of change in attitudes toward public policy, it is difficult to isolate the various sources of influence.

LIBERALISM - CONSERVATISM

Most commentators on the American political scene—not to mention the active participants—describe much of what happens in terms of liberalism and conservatism. Political history (and current news analysis) is portrayed as "trends of liberalism," "middle-of-the-road policies," "rejection of conservatism." Analysts characterize candidates and political parties as liberal and conservative; within each party leaders and platforms are alleged to be relatively liberal and conservative. The major problem is to assess the importance of this variable in mass public

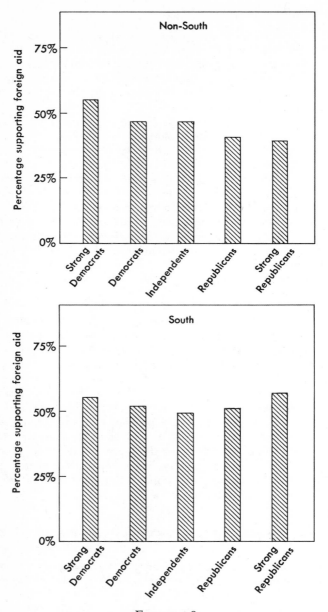

FIGURE 4.8
Support for Foreign Aid in 1964 According to
Region and Partisanship.

Source: Survey Research Center, University of Michigan.

opinion and more specifically to decide if individuals in society are self-consciously oriented to politics as liberals, middle-of-the-roaders, or conservatives, and to determine whether individuals use this ideological orientation to organize political information and attitudes. In other words, does political ideology play a role for Americans similar to the role of partisanship as a basic determinant of their specific political views?

Survey Research Center data reported in *The American Voter* show that very few members of the electorate discuss their evaluations of the parties and the candidates in ideological language, fewer than 15 percent in 1956.[3] While the incidence of words like "liberal" and "conservative" in the voters' discussions during campaigns like 1964 would be higher presumably than in 1956, *the overwhelming weight of evidence indicates that most voters do not evaluate candidates or select their political parties in conformity with an ideological commitment.* As with other political ideas in the minds of Americans, political ideologies are vague, superficial labels applied rather indifferently in their environment.

On the other hand when Americans are asked to identify themselves as liberals or conservatives, they are able to do so. The categories obviously have some meaning for most Americans; the categories simply are not of over-riding importance. According to this uncomplicated measure of self-identification the electorate is about one-third middle-of-the-road, one-third liberal and one-third conservative. Unfortunately no major political studies of public opinion in the United States have used ideological self-identification as a basis of explanation or for purposes of descriptions, so it is impossible to compare the impact of ideological identification on political attitudes with the impact of partisan identification.

Some analysts have attempted to create measures of liberalism-conservatism from answers to questions on public policy. Several general conclusions can be drawn from these efforts. First, in the national electorate there is not a strong, consistent ordering of individuals on a liberal-conservative dimension if a large number of specific public policies are used. Or to put it differently *Americans are not consistently liberal, conservative or moderate on a wide range of issues.* A given individual will be liberal on farm issues, conservative on labor union issues, moderate on education, and so on. A second individual will be liberal on labor matters, moderate on education and conservative on farm policy. When viewed collectively, these individuals' opinions form no single consistent pattern even though each individual's attitudes might be reasonable enough for him. Since it is likely that many individual responses to questions of public policy have little meaning or

[3] Angus Campbell, *et al.*, *The American Voter*, p. 249.

salience for the individual, *the absence of a strong liberal-conservative dimension on issues reflects the unimportance of the issues for the electorate.*

As the range of issues narrows, the positions taken by the public show less variation and inconsistency. A fairly stable attitude dimension on welfare policies and government economic activity has been documented in *The American Voter*.[4] Although this domestic economic activity measure is related to party identification (Democrats are more liberal; Republicans are more conservative), *domestic economic issue positions are not related to attitudes on other domestic issues or attitudes toward foreign policy.* Table 4.2 from V. O. Key's *Public Opinion and*

TABLE 4.2   *Relation of Position on Domestic Liberalism Scale to Position on Internationalism Scale, 1956. (Survey Research Center, University of Michigan.)*

INTERNATIONALISM	LIBERALISM		
	Low	Medium	High
High	50%	59%	58%
Medium	32	28	21
Low	18	13	21
Total	100%	100%	100%
n =	226	598	491

Source: V. O. Key, Jr., *Public Opinion and American Democracy* (New York: Alfred A. Knopf, 1961), p. 158, Table 7.2.

American Democracy shows the common pattern of no relationship between liberalism-conservatism and internationalism-isolationism. The two dimensions appear quite independent of one another in the general public even though the dimensions may be interrelated among political leaders.

Attitudes toward public policies are influenced by several factors:

1) Some individuals undoubtedly take stands on issues in order to be consistent with a general ideological position or to be consistent with a general ideological position or to be consistent with a general commitment like opposition to federal government programs or support for military aid to non-communist countries.

2) Some individuals take a stand on an issue to be consistent with their political party or to agree with a political leader whom they support.

3) Some individuals favor or oppose a policy because they believe they have important interests at stake.

    [4] Angus Campbell, *et al.*, *The American Voter*, pp. 194–97.

If everyone had a strong ideology, their attitudes would be determined by their ideology. To a considerable extent this appears to happen to the most politically alert and concerned in our society, but this group is only a very small minority of the total adult population. If our major political parties were ideologically oriented, then by following the parties or political leaders in our parties Americans would have their opinions determined indirectly by ideology. But our two major political parties are notoriously non-ideological—many of the leaders have personal ideological commitments, but no single ideology dominates the parties. Finally neither ideology nor party loyalty is important enough for most people to determine their attitudes toward policy if they believe extremely important interests are at stake. In fact most Americans ignore ideology and misperceive their party's position if they hold a strong view on a public policy, and if they discover that their party or ideology is in conflict with their interests, Americans weaken their support of their usual party or ideology.

Usually specific matters of public policy are of little interest to the electorate and the political parties are unconcerned with dramatizing particular policies. Under these circumstances most attitudes toward public policies are extremely casual views. It is relatively unusual in American politics for an issue to become so important that it disrupts party loyalties for large numbers of people. *But in the rare case when individuals feel important interests are at stake, it is most unlikely that party loyalty or ideological beliefs will overcome strongly felt interests.*

LIBERALISM AND CONSERVATISM AS PERSONALITY FACTORS

Due mainly to the work of Herbert McClosky the liberalism-conservatism dimension has been applied in political analysis in a way not directly related to public policy or political parties. In his "Conservatism and Personality,"[5] McClosky developed an index of liberalism-conservatism that measures personality or individual style. McClosky documented a wide array of relationships between psychological variables and liberalism-conservatism. His findings suggest that there are basic orientations toward governmental activity and the nature of society which could under the right circumstances influence political behavior. These personality measures of liberalism-conservatism are not associated with Democratic and Republican party loyalty or voting behavior. Of course, there is no reason to expect personality factors to be associated with party loyalty or vote choice or public policy views,

[5] Herbert McClosky, "Conservatism and Personality," *American Political Science Review*, Vol. 52 (March 1958), pp. 27–45.

but this means that the applications of McClosky's work are somewhat limited to date.[6]

Two other major attempts to relate personality characteristics to political behavior should be mentioned. Extremist political beliefs and activities have been a central concern of social scientists even though in American society extremists are a tiny fraction of the whole society. Extremist groups draw members from all parts of society. In particular, right-wing extremists like the John Birch Society appear to have members of high social status; groups like the Ku Klux Klan and the Black Muslims have members of low social status. More important, individuals attracted to extremist groups are likely to have a cluster of atypical personality characteristics including anxiety, hostility and insecurity. These generalizations must be considered highly tentative since there are only a few studies of extremists in American society.[7]

A different approach to the study of ideology and personality has been launched by Robert Lane.[8] His efforts to show that individual political styles and beliefs are based on personality characteristics have been limited to a small number of cases and the results cannot be extended easily to the American public. Nevertheless Lane demonstrates that many elements of ideological belief and political style have psychological roots.

CONSENSUS ON RULES OF THE GAME

One further element of public opinion to be considered is the nature of support in the American political system for fundamental principles of a democratic society. A widely held and perfectly plausible belief is that the American public supports free speech for all, free elections, civil rights, and other operating rules of a democratic society. At a highly abstract level this is true enough. American citizens ascribe to the basic rules of democracy overwhelmingly when this commitment is kept vague and abstract. As individuals are asked about more and more precise applications of democratic principles, agreement disappears. Specifically there is not widespread agreement in the American electorate on extending civil rights and liberties to individuals with unpopular political and social opinions.

[6] Survey Research Center data show that individuals who shift political parties are distributed in such a way that those who shift toward the Republican Party are more likely to be conservative; those who shift toward the Democratic Party are less likely to be conservative.

[7] The major study in recent years is Daniel Bell, *The Radical Right* (New York: Doubleday Anchor Books, 1964).

[8] Robert Lane, *Political Ideology* (New York: The Free Press of Glencoe, 1962).

Two important qualifications are in order. First, the electorate's responses are attitudes which may have little meaning for them and are not measures of their behavior or even measures of their attitudes under circumstances of great concern for democratic principles. Furthermore, while it is apparently true that large numbers of Americans do not support democratic rules for all citizens, it does not necessarily follow that these same large numbers would support the denial of civil rights and liberties when faced with that alternative. Nevertheless it is a remarkable failure of American political education and socialization that there is not more firm support for the specific applications of American democratic traditions.

The second important qualification of these findings applies to the political, social and economic leaders in American society who consistently support these democratic principles more strongly than the general public. Usually support among leaders is so high that it is possible to conclude that the leaders in society defend and maintain democratic procedures. The leaders' consensus on democratic rights and values makes the weakness of the general public less crucial. National studies by Stouffer[9] and McClosky[10] support the view that leaders are stronger in support of rules-of-the-game than the public. Table 4.3 from McClosky's study shows the degree to which leaders support the rules-of-the-game in comparison with the public. Political influentials, in this study delegates and alternates to the Democratic and Republican national conventions in 1956, are consistently more likely to agree with rules-of-the-game than a sample of the electorate. It may not be reassuring to discover that 6.8 per cent of the political influentials agree that "the majority has the right to abolish minorities if it wants to" or that 13.3 per cent agree that "almost any unfairness or brutality may have to be justified when some great purpose is being carried out." But in both examples substantially greater proportions, one-quarter and one-third respectively, of the general electorate support these views. Presumably leaders are recruited and educated in such a way that they come prepared with or develop agreement on democratic procedures. Apparently leaders make decisions in society in a number of ways which maintain democratic practices even without widespread public support.

The widespread interest in public opinion and rules-of-the-game has been based partly on two somewhat mistaken impressions. First, the popular concern with public attitudes on policy issues is based

[9] Samuel Stouffer, *Communism, Conformity and Civil Liberties* (New York: Doubleday, 1955).

[10] Herbert McClosky, "Consensus and Ideology in American Politics," *American Political Science Review*, Vol. 58 (June 1964), pp. 361–82.

TABLE 4.3   *Political Influentials vs. the Electorate: Response to Items Expressing "Rules of the Game"**

ITEMS	POLITICAL INFLUENTIALS	GENERAL ELECTORATE
There are times when it almost seems better for the people to take the law into their own hands rather than wait for the machinery of government to act.	13.3%	26.9%
The majority has the right to abolish minorities if it wants to.	6.8%	28.4%
We might as well make up our minds that in order to make the world better a lot of innocent people will have to suffer.	27.2%	41.6%
If Congressional committees stuck strictly to the rules and gave every witness his rights, they would never succeed in exposing the many dangerous subversives they have turned up.	24.7%	47.4%
I don't mind a politician's methods if he manages to get the right things done.	25.6%	42.4%
Almost any unfairness or brutality may have to be justified when some great purpose is being carried out.	13.3%	32.8%
Politicians have to cut a few corners if they are going to get anywhere.	29.4%	43.2%
People ought to be allowed to vote even if they can't do so intelligently.	65.6%	47.6%
To bring about great changes for the benefit of mankind often requires cruelty and even ruthlessness.	19.4%	31.3%
Very few politicians have clean records, so why get excited about the mud-slinging that sometimes goes on?	14.8%	38.1%
It is all right to get around the law if you don't actually break it.	21.2%	30.2%
The true American way of life is disappearing so fast that we may have to use force to save it.	12.8%	34.6%
n =	3020	1484

* Since respondents were forced to make a choice on each item, the number of omitted or "don't know" responses was, on the average, fewer than one percent, and thus has little influence on the direction or magnitude of the results reported in this table.

Source: Herbert McClosky, "Consensus and Ideology in American Politics," in Dreyer and Rosenbaum, eds., *Public Opinion and Electoral Behavior* (Belmont, California: Wadsworth Publishing Co., 1966), p. 243, Table 1.

partially on the assumption that the public influences the making of policy, but actually we now believe that the public has little influence on policy formation and that on most matters public opinion follows policy-making. The study of public opinion has not proved to be a significant aspect of policy-making studies. Second, there has been an assumption that stable democratic political systems rest on a nearly universal commitment to fundamental principles and their application, but the evidence on this point is inconclusive. Certainly a democratic system cannot long survive widespread, intense hostility, but probably the positive belief in particular operating procedures among the public is unnecessary. Hostility to democratic procedures is fatal whether among the leaders or the public, but support of these procedures may prove essential only among leaders. Perhaps the public need not agree on basic principles so long as it does not demand disruptive policies and procedures.

In a different perspective the failure of public opinion to be as important as expected in these respects is a failure of the American political system to conform to simple democratic ideals as developed in political theory. Democratic theory has given public opinion a prominent role, more prominent than found in reality. But this portrayal is not so much a dissent from democratic theory as it is a realization that democratic theory has focused on negative and supportive opinions, those rare circumstances in which the public demands a policy. But in fact policy disputes are almost always over matters of indifference to the public, the realm of permissive opinion. These findings follow from the basic indifference of Americans to politics and public policies and represent an abandonment of the role assigned the public in democratic theory, a role calling for considerably greater interest, information and vigilance. But in truth the high degree of concern postulated for the public in democratic theory may only accompany social and political crises of such intensity that democracy itself is in jeopardy. It has been argued that the political indifference of Americans is a sign of social and economic health.

This conclusion would be more comforting if it were not suspected that these configurations of opinion were a basic weakness in our political system. Specifically the public provides support for the political leaders, and the ignorance and apathy in leaders' followings is a potential weakness. A leader's following is vulnerable to irrelevant and inappropriate appeals. The following's failure to understand policy and rules-of-the-game means they cannot be counted on to support the leader on the basis of policies or principles. Under the worst circumstances democratic leaders might lose support to undemocratic leaders without the followers realizing what was happening. Less dramatically, and doubtless more commonly, leaders who support policies beneficial to their following lose support to leaders whose policies are inappropriate for the following on the basis of some irrelevant and insignificant issue.

In the last chapter the role of issues in support of candidates in elections is considered, and this is the most likely form of influence by the public over policy.

chapter 5

Campaigns and Electoral Decisions

MOST AMERICANS BECOME SUFFICIENTLY CONCERNED WITH PRESI-
dential elections and even state and local elections to be interested in
finding out who wins and to pay attention to highlights of the campaigns. Undeniably American political campaigns are an extraordinary
set of practices. For all the foolishness and viciousness occasionally
present during a campaign, elections are an important method of arousing public interest in politics and issues and a most important technique
for selecting and rejecting political leaders. Political campaigns have
several purposes.

1) to increase turnout for candidates or a referendum;
2) to publicize the attractive qualities of candidates, platforms and per-
   formance; and
3) to raise money and to recruit workers for the campaign.

The payoff for these efforts is victory on election day. It is desirable
to assess the nature and impact of campaign activities.

CAMPAIGN PARTICIPATION

The greatest spectacle of American politics, the Presidential campaign
and election, involves about four million workers in telephoning, door-
bell ringing, addressing envelopes, and doing the work of the campaign.
While this is a large number, it is fewer people than participate
annually in amateur theatricals or engage in almost any other kind of
volunteer activity. A rather small proportion of American citizens is

attracted to campaign work, considering the crucial role of elections in our political system. As Table 5.1 shows, there was a slight increase in campaign workers during the period from 1952 to 1964. While there is considerable overlap among individuals in each of these categories, the percentages do not represent the same set of individuals. For example, many individuals who contribute financially are not

TABLE 5.1 *Campaign Activities in 1952, 1956, 1960 and 1964.*

	1952	1956	1960	1964
Do you belong to any political club or organization?	2%	3%	3%	4%
Did you give any money or buy tickets or anything to help the campaign for one of the parties or candidates?	4%	10%	11%	11%
Did you go to any political meetings, rallies, dinners, or things like that?	7%	7%	8%	8%
Did you do any other work for one of the parties or candidates?	3%	3%	5%	5%

Source: Survey Research Center, University of Michigan.

involved in the campaign in any other way. It is somewhat surprising to confirm a finding reported originally by Robert Salisbury that over half of the members of political clubs and organizations are not currently involved in any campaign activity.[1] So *counting all forms of campaign activity well over 10 per cent of the electorate are involved in some way.*

The increase of campaign activity has been greater among Republicans than Democrats or independents during this twelve-year period. By 1964 a large proportion of strongly partisan Republicans were giving money (about one-third) and attending meetings or rallies (about one-quarter) while among Democrats, independents, and less partisan Republicans less than one-tenth were active in these ways. In part these distributions are a result of the higher socio-economic position of Republicans; campaign contributions, for example, come disproportionately from the well-to-do. Higher income individuals cannot only better afford to give, they are easier to locate for solicitation.

[1] Robert Salisbury, "The Urban Party Organization Member," *Public Opinion Quarterly*, Vol. XXIX (Winter 1965–66), p. 553.

Also, in 1964 the depletion of the ranks of strong Republicans in reaction against the Goldwater candidacy left a group of more highly committed and active followers. Although strong Republicans were fewer in number, they were more likely to engage in campaign activities in support of their party. The Republican Party advantage in campaign activity shows up most clearly in fund raising. Not only do Republican ranks include a majority of the most wealthy in our society, the Republican Party contacts many more people than the Democrats for fund raising and receives contributions from many more. The result is that nationally the Republican Party raises more money through campaign solicitation than the Democratic Party.

On the other hand, Democrats have about as many campaign actives as the Republicans since there are so many more Democrats from which actives can be drawn. The Republicans still have more contributors, meeting-goers, and campaign workers but the differences are not great. Table 5.2 shows how campaign workers in different

TABLE 5.2   *The Active Campaign Workers of 1964 According to Partisanship and Their Preference for President.*

| | VOTED FOR | | NON-VOTER WHO PREFERRED | |
	JOHNSON	GOLDWATER	JOHNSON	GOLDWATER
Strong Democrat	21%		1	
Democrat	8	3	1	
Independent	3	5		
Republican	7	11		1
Strong Republican	1	36		
Apolitical		1		
Subtotal	40%	56%	2%	1%
Total		99%		
n =		58		

Source: Survey Research Center, University of Michigan.

partisanship categories were distributed in their preference for President in 1964. For whom or to what purpose these individuals campaigned is not known, but it is likely that almost all worked for the same party as their Presidential vote. Goldwater appears to have had more supporters actively involved in campaign work than Johnson. Although more campaign activity centers around Presidential candidates than other candidates, the Presidential race does not dominate the campaign to the exclusion of other races and general activity on behalf of the parties. In recent campaigns the relative advantage in numbers of workers enjoyed by the Republican Party does not appear to be overwhelming. As discussion below will suggest, the advantage Goldwater may have had in numbers (and perhaps in enthusiasm) of campaign workers in 1964 could not have overcome Johnson's overall advantage among the voters in a race that was lost for all practical purposes before the campaign started.

IMPACT OF POLITICAL CAMPAIGNS

A question that cannot be ignored is the impact of party activities and political campaigns generally on the American electorate. Although most professional politicians take for granted the efficacy of campaigns, scholarly analysis has often questioned their impact. For example, some campaigns to promote and publicize political ideas have had little impact. Furthermore, in most elections the overwhelming majority of voters decide how they will vote before the campaign begins. Beyond this the general low level of political information in the American electorate throws doubt on the ability of voters to absorb ideas during a campaign.

Perhaps two aspects of the problem should be distinguished in assessing the impact of political campaigns. First, there is the overall impact on the total electorate, and the evidence indicates that *most voters are not affected by political campaigns*. Second, there is the possibility that campaigning influences a small but crucial proportion of the electorate, and *many elections are close enough that the winning margin could be a result of the campaign*. It seems clear that professional politicians drive themselves and their organizations to influence every remaining undecided voter in the hope and expectation that they are providing or maintaining a winning margin.

One way of approaching the problem of campaign impact is to see how many voters make up their minds before the campaign starts. Table 5.3 shows that in Presidential elections from 1948 to 1954 voters made their vote choice at about the same time for most elections, and in most years about one-third of the electorate decided before the conventions, another one-third decided during the conventions, and a final one-third decided during the campaign. In 1956 the rematch between Stevenson and an extremely popular Eisenhower was the most deviant election, where well over half of the voters made a decision on how they would vote before the conventions. Partisan differences between Democrats and Republicans are shown in Figure 5.1. In 1948 and 1960, the only close elections during the period, the Democrats won the election by coming from behind during the campaign period. In

TABLE 5.3 *Distribution of Time of Decision on Vote Choice for President in 1948, 1952, 1956, 1960 and 1964.*

	1948	1952	1956	1960	1964
Decided					
Before conventions	37%	35%	57%	30%	40%
During conventions	22	39	18	30	25
During campaign	26	31	21	36	33
Don't remember, NA	9	4	4	4	3
Total	100%	101%	100%	100%	101%
n =	421	1251	1285	1445	1126

Source: Survey Research Center, University of Michigan.

those years, the Republicans had leads of 53 to 47 and 56 to 44 at the start of the campaigns, so Democrats overcame substantial leads in both elections. In 1952, 1956 and 1964 the eventual losers could not overcome leads of 60 to 40, 60 to 40 and 73 to 27. By the end of the conventions in 1956 and 1964, more voters had decided in favor of Eisenhower and Johnson, respectively, than their opponents would have by election day. In the extremely one-sided elections the winner's advantage accrues early, and during their respective campaigns Eisenhower and Johnson did not win substantially more additional voters to their side than their opponents.

There are also differences in the decision times of partisans and independents because the "safe" party vote lines up early behind the party's candidate. A fairly persistent pattern of time of decision is shown in Table 5.4. In both 1960 and 1964 the independents and weak partisans were more likely to make up their minds during the campaign while the strong partisans characteristically made their decisions earlier. To put it differently the less committed are still undecided at the start of the campaign. *In fairly close elections this relatively uncommitted group can still swing the election either way, but in one-sided contests those who are still undecided during the campaign are too few in number to change the outcome.*

It is widely reported that the most interested voters make their vote decisions early and that the least interested voters remain undecided during the campaign. A great deal has been made of this generalization and its implications for campaign strategy. Essentially the consideration has taken this form: the least interested (and least concerned and least informed) are the only voters still available during the campaign, and in order to influence them, very simple campaign appeals are necessary. The interested voters (mainly partisan and already com-

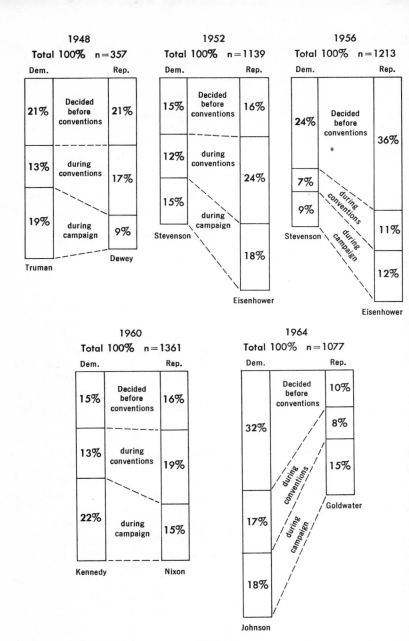

FIGURE 5.1

Distribution of Democratic and Republican Votes for President According to Time of Decision for 1948–1964.

Source: Survey Research Center, University of Michigan.

TABLE 5.4 *Distribution of Time of Decision of Vote Choice for President in 1960 and 1964 According to Partisanship.*

	STRONG DEMO-CRAT	1960 DEMO-CRAT	INDE-PENDENT	REPUB-LICAN	STRONG REPUB-LICAN
Decided Before convention	41%	24%	24%	29%	38%
During convention	31	24	28	28	48
During campaign	28	52	48	43	15
Total	100%	100%	100%	100%	100%
n =	296	325	292	205	241

		1964			
Decided Before convention	59%	38%	30%	29%	36%
During convention	24	26	23	25	30
During campaign	17	36	47	46	34
Total	100%	100%	100%	100%	100%
n =	311	258	217	159	140

Source: Survey Research Center, University of Michigan.

mitted) are held in line with appeals to party loyalty. This description is appropriate for some recent campaigns, but it is not necessarily a permanent characteristic of the American electorate. In fact the above description fits only the Eisenhower elections and perhaps the later Roosevelt elections. In 1960 there was a slight tendency for the least interested voters to decide early rather than late, and in 1964 there was no difference in the time of decision of the most interested and least interested. In other words under some circumstances interested voters are as likely as uninterested voters to enter the campaign still undecided on their vote choice. This is not to say that these interested voters are completely without preferences or that they are extremely well informed. They are neither. But *it is not true that in all political campaigns the only voters still undecided at the start of the campaign are uninterested in politics.*

IMPACT OF PARTY CONTACT

One of the most direct attempts to influence voters is through door-to-door solicitation and telephoning. The reported impact of these efforts by party workers through personal contact is not impressive. Almost all voters report that they have not been influenced in their vote choice by party contacts. However, party contact may influence turnout and the level of financial contributions to the party. Since 1952 there has been a steady increase in the proportion of the electorate reporting they have been contacted personally by one or both parties— from 11 per cent in 1952 to 17 per cent in 1956 to 20 percent in 1960 to 26 per cent in 1964. The increase—about fifteen million more voters contacted in 1964 than in 1952—represents an enormous effort by party organizations. Whether it has much impact or not, personal contact is an activity which political organizations without great wealth can deliver, and since there is some evidence of payoff, it is an activity not likely to be abandoned. This evidence consists of findings which show that the party vote is somewhat greater than expected in areas of exceptional efforts in contacting voters.

MASS MEDIA AND POLITICAL CAMPAIGNS

At least as important as personal party contact during a political campaign is the contact made by candidates and party leaders through the mass media, mainly newspaper, radio and television. Political information is transmitted by the mass media in two ways: through news stories and through advertising. There is no basis for assessing the relative impact of news versus advertising by the various media in political campaigns. Actually political scientists have seldom studied the impact of the content of the mass media, and in part this neglect is a reflection of the belief that campaigns are unimportant, that elections are decided before the campaign starts. Beyond this there is the belief that American voters have little political information from the mass media or from any other source.

Several familiar patterns of attention are paid to the mass media. Individuals most interested in and concerned about politics pay greatest attention to politics in the mass media. Beyond this the better educated and the higher socio-economic groups pay greater attention to the mass media as a source of political information. Also there is a tendency for strong partisans to pay more attention to the mass media than other members of the electorate.

In social science by far the most important generalization about media attention has to do with "selective perception." Selective perception refers to a tendency to select information that conforms to one's ideas and values. Individuals allegedly avoid media content that would conflict with their present point of view and seek out information that reinforces their views. In the terms used in Chapter 4 an individual selectively perceives mass media content in order to avoid or reduce dissonance. It is persuasive to argue that Democrats are more likely than Republicans to read news stories about Democratic candidates or to watch a Democratic television commercial. Common sense —if not empirical evidence—suggests that something like this does occur. However, there is no factual basis for believing that most voters successfully avoid political information that is in conflict with their present views. Most Americans are unavoidably exposed to political ideas and values with which they do not agree.

A clear example of a case in which selective perception almost certainly did not operate is the 1960 television debates between Kennedy and Nixon, when it would have been practically impossible to ignore one candidate and pay attention to the other. The debates illustrate the substantial impact that can come through the mass media under the right circumstances. Nearly everyone in the American electorate watched one or more television debates and according to several different public opinion polls about half of the voters reported they were influenced by the debates in their evaluation of the candidates. Several millions of voters reported that they based their choice of candidates solely on the debates. Among voters reporting that the debates determined their vote choice, Kennedy held an advantage of three to one over Nixon.

No other opportunity in recent campaigns for winning so many uncommitted voters or winning over voters inclined to one's opponent has compared with the television debates of 1960. However, another significant political opportunity is the party nominating convention every four years. An increasingly large television audience is available to each party during the conventions but it appears difficult to hold the attention of the audience for extended periods of time, particularly if there is no contest for the Presidential nomination. Furthermore, the strong partisans follow their party's convention more intently than other members of the electorate.

In 1964, for the first time in recent Presidential elections, books and political pamphlets were prominent. Many millions of volumes were sold or given away during the campaign, mainly by supporters of Barry Goldwater. We have no indication of the impact of this material and no way as yet of assessing the immediate and long run influence of these materials.

The impact of mass media exposure on voting behavior in recent elections has been studied by Philip Converse of the Survey Research Center and he draws several conclusions based on the findings like those represented in Figure 5.2.[2] The most stable voters (whether

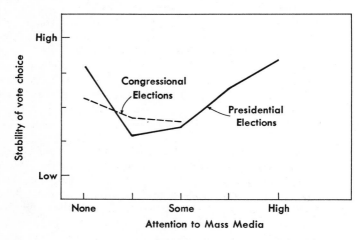

FIGURE 5.2

The Hypothetical Relationship between Mass Media Attention and Stability of Voting Behavior.

stability is measured as during a campaign or between elections) are those who are highly attentive to mass media and those who pay no attention to media communication. *The shifting, unstable voters are more likely to be moderately exposed to mass media.* To restate this pattern: the least involved voters who receive no information from the mass media remain stable in their vote choice because no new information is introduced to change their vote. Their apathy and their lack of information protect them from forces which would alter their political preferences. The most involved voters who expose themselves to mass media and pay considerable attention to politics are sufficiently well informed and secure in their vote choice that some new information does not alter their commitment. The shifting voters are moderately involved in politics and moderately exposed to mass media, but seem-

[2] Philip Converse, "Information Flow and the Stability of Partisan Attitudes," *Public Opinion Quarterly*, Vol. XXVI (Winter 1962), pp. 578–99.

ingly new information can have a substantial impact on their vote choice since their commitment is less intense. To be sure, the less involved and less attentive an individual is, the less likely he is to bother to vote at all, so the above relationship applies only to those who do happen to vote. In non-Presidential elections several differences can be anticipated. Large numbers of citizens are exposed to no mass media and there are much larger numbers of non-voters. At the other end of the curve there are fewer people with high media attention since so much less mass media content is devoted to non-Presidential campaigns. In effect in "low salience" elections there are two types of media exposure, some and none, and voting instability is about the same in both categories.

OPINION LEADERSHIP

Still another aspect of the communication of political information is face-to-face discussion of ideas and values in the general public. Not much is known about the communication of political ideas through casual discussions with friends, family members, and fellow workers, but there is a widespread belief among social scientists that face-to-face communication accounts for much of the learning and reinforcing of political views in our society.

This social process of political communication is not difficult to describe but it would be enormously difficult to investigate. It is mere speculation that opinion leadership exists in the following form on political subjects. Supposedly political ideas are transmitted in what is often called a "two-step flow of communication" from opinion elites (leaders in the society like politicians, businessmen, news commentators) to a minority of the public, opinion leaders, who in turn transmit the ideas on to the remainder of the public. Graphically the process looks like this:

For example, E_1 who might be a news commentator or a political leader communicates through the mass media a set of ideas. Some members of the public like P_1 receive the communication directly and that is the end of it, but other members of the public like L_1 not only receive a message from E_1 but pass it on to others, P_2, P_3, and P_4. Some members of the public like P_2 receive the communication directly from E_1 and indirectly from E_1 through an opinion leader, L_1. P_3 has only one source of information on this topic, an opinion leader, L_1; and P_4 has two sources of information, L_1 and L_2, both opinion leaders. Some opinion leaders like L_3 have several sources of information in the opinion elite. Some individuals like N_1 receive no information on the topic directly or indirectly.

On major political subjects there are supposedly thousands of individuals in the opinion elite; that is, there are thousands of individuals communicating impersonally to large audiences through the mass media. The number of opinion leaders undoubtedly varies from subject to subject. On topics like Kennedy's assassination or the Viet Nam war most members of the public pass on information to someone else so that under extreme circumstances everyone may serve as an opinion leader. At the other extreme there may be so little attention to a subject that almost no one acts as an opinion leader and most individuals are non-participants, outside the flow of communication. On topics like farm subsidies or school desegregation or admission of Communist China to the United Nations it is not known how many opinion leaders there are in society nor is it known how much influence they have on the opinions of the people who listen to them. During Presidential political campaigns over one-fourth of the electorate self-consciously attempts to influence others with respect to their vote choice, but their success has never been investigated. Furthermore it is not known how many people have influence as opinion leaders without being aware of it. In the face of these difficulties the following speculation is hazardous at best.

Opinion leaders are not much different socially and economically from the individuals they influence. There may be a tendency for them to be slightly better educated and slightly higher in socio-economic status, but there are opinion leaders in all parts of society. Opinion leaders are almost certainly more interested in politics and better informed than the individuals they influence. There may be subject specialization by opinion leaders in some groups and in other groups politics may be of such low salience that there is no opportunity for specialized opinion leadership. Some opinion leaders may transmit the information they receive faithfully without distortion. It seems more likely that opinion leaders add and subtract information and reinterpret it for their following. Some opinion leaders probably tailor their ideas to the expectations of their following, always telling them what they

TABLE 5.5 Total Number of References to Characteristics of Republican and Democratic Presidential Candidates, 1952–1964.[a] (Survey Research Center, University of Michigan)

References	1952		1956		1960		1964	
	Eisen-hower	Steven-son	Eisen-hower	Steven-son	Nixon	Ken-nedy	Gold-water	John-son
Positive	3153	2154	3485	1703	2790	2678	1505	3271
Negative	1415	1243	1378	1567	1214	1836	2815	1463
n =	1798		1761		1807		1570	

[a] The data in this table have been adjusted to remove the effect of differences in the number of respondents in the four surveys. The 1960 sample was taken as the base.

Source: Angus Campbell, "Interpreting the Presidential Victory," in M. Cummings, ed., The National Election of 1964 (Washington: Brookings Institution, 1966), p. 259, Table 8.1.

want to hear, and reinforcing their convictions and beliefs about reality. Other opinion leaders may frequently introduce new and perhaps disquieting ideas and evaluations. Under some conditions this may lead either to confusion and alienation or to an adjustment of individuals' opinions to new conditions. In consumer research and some commercial advertising campaigns, efforts have been made to locate and appeal to opinion leaders as a way of publicizing or spreading a product. No comparable efforts have been made in political campaigning, partly because no one knows how to locate or appeal to the opinion leaders of uncommitted voters.

CANDIDATE IMAGE AND POLITICAL CAMPAIGNS

Variable, short-run influences on voting choice do not appear to determine as many votes as do stable influences like partisanship. On the other hand these short-run influences cause the deviations from the basic party division and the deviation may determine the outcome of an election. One measure of short-run influences is the response to candidates during recent campaigns. As Table 5.5 shows, in 1952 and 1956 Eisenhower was much more favorably perceived by the electorate than Stevenson and this advantage is one explanation for Eisenhower's victory in an electorate with more Democrats than Republicans. In 1964 not only did Johnson have the usual Democratic advantage in basic strength but he was much more favorably viewed by the voters than Goldwater. Goldwater was the only candidate in the four recent Presidential elections to be viewed more negatively than positively by the electorate. The 1960 election shows the short-run candidate image favoring Nixon over Kennedy rather strongly but this was not enough for the Republican candidate to overcome the basic Democratic advantage.

The specific content of the candidates' image has varied greatly and no single pattern appears associated with either party. For example, a large proportion of the favorable and unfavorable references to Eisenhower in 1952 had to do with his experience as a military man, but by 1956 he was perceived almost entirely in other terms, mainly personal qualities rather than experience or qualifications. In 1964 the only strong point in Goldwater's image was "integrity" whereas many unfavorable references were made to his personal characteristics like "impulsiveness" and "trigger happy" and to his stands on issues. In 1960 Nixon's advantage over Kennedy rested mainly on a more favorable public impression of his qualifications and experience and an unfavorable reaction by many to Kennedy's Catholicism.

The candidates and their policy positions influence vote choices indirectly through issues. Table 5.6 shows the changing perception of the parties in handling foreign affairs and emphasizes the loss by Re-

TABLE 5.6 *Perceptions as to the Party Most Likely to Keep the United States out of War in the Ensuing Four Years. (Survey Research Center, University of Michigan)*

	1956	1960	1964
Democrats would handle better	7%	15%	38%
No party difference	45	46	46
Republicans would handle better	40	29	12
Don't know, not ascertained	8	10	4
Total	100%	100%	100%

Source: P. Converse, A. Clausen and W. Miller, "Electoral Myth and Realty" in E. Dreyer and W. Rosenbaum, eds., *Political Opinion and Electoral Behavior Essays and Studies* (Belmont, Calif.: Wadsworth Publishing Co., 1966), p. 28, Table 1.

publican Presidential candidates of their greatest asset in contests with Democrats. (It is this advantage that Republicans appear to be regaining since 1964 as a consequence of the Viet Nam war.) The candidates, after all, campaign on the issues more or less; *the only determinants of vote choice which the candidates can manipulate during the campaign are the issue stands they take and the relative emphasis given the issues.*

Several characteristics of electoral behavior conflict with this description of the role of issues in influencing vote choice. For one thing in most elections many voters are unaware of the stands taken by candidates on issues. It is common to find that voters believe the candidates they support agree with them on issues, and so voters may project their issue positions onto their favorite candidate more often than they decide to vote for a candidate on the basis of his position on issues. Furthermore when voters agree on issues with the candidate they support, they may have adopted this position merely in order to agree with their candidate. Actually candidates and other political leaders frequently perform this function for members of the electorate; *they provide issue leadership for their following.*

There are limits to the issue influence and to appreciate the role of issues, their importance to individual voters must be considered. Figure 5.3 displays the possibilities. Situation I is relatively uncommon in American elections, an election in which an issue (or issues) so dominates the electorate that issue stands by candidates determine the outcome. What is more likely, however, is that small collections of voters will care intensely about different issues and some of these may, indeed, support whichever candidate is closest to their position. In

Individual A's concern for issue X initially	Individual A's view of candidate B's stand on issue X	Candidate B's influence over Individual A on issue X	Impact of Issue X on electorate
I. Issue X of great importance to Individual A	Individual A cares so much that he will find out how Candidate B stands on Issue X.	Candidate B has little influence over Individual A and he will not be able to conceal his position on Issue X.	Individuals will oppose or support a candidate because of his stand on Issue X. If all individuals are deeply concerned with Issue X, it will have a great impact on voting.
II. Issue X of some interest to Individual A	Individual A may misperceive Candidate B's stand on Issue X or he may be informed of his stand.	Candidate B may change Individual A's position on Issue X or he may lead Individual A to think Issue X is more significant.	Issue X will not influence voting because individuals will learn their stand from a candidate they already support or support a candidate with a stand contrary to their own.
III. Issue X of no importance to Individual A	Individual A will neither know nor care about Candidate B's stand on Issue X.	Candidate B will not be able to influence Individual A nor will he be able to get Individual A to pay attention to Issue X.	Issue X will not influence turnout or votes for candidates. Even if the candidates treat Issue X as significant, it will not be consequential.

FIGURE 5.3

Categories of Response to Issues and Candidates and Their Impact on the Electorate.

almost all elections a very small minority of voters is expected to vote on the basis of any single issue. Exceptional issues may create situations in which an election can be won with a single issue. The classic issue of American politics for achieving this has been the cluster of issues associated with the legacy of the Civil War sometimes called the "bloody shirt." Currently the many matters associated with the "race issue" have this impact on large numbers of voters in some constituencies. Candidates for public office are usually searching for issues of this type which will help them. It is this constant search for such issues by the politically ambitious which leads to the assertion that in a democracy intense interests in the electorate cannot be long ignored.

Situation III, complete indifference to some issue, is quite common among the enormous range of topics that might be considered issues at any given time. A great many issues that are important to political leaders remain in this category for the general public. It has been particularly frustrating for American political leaders since World War II that the public has taken so little interest in foreign affairs. In general American voters are assumed to care about domestic economic issues, if they care about any issue, and to be indifferent to foreign policy issues. A related but different emphasis casts this relationship in a broader pattern: *voters care intensely about an issue when they are suffering or perceive a threat* and usually the easiest threat to understand is economic; the most difficult to comprehend are in the areas of foreign policy. Situation II falls somewhere in between the two extremes and applies to the few, major issues of an ordinary campaign. The individual voters can be aroused to take a stand on the issue in support of their party or candidate and be made to care moderately about the issue. The voters recognize its importance but do not feel a great personal stake in the matter.

A major aspect of the Survey Research Center analysis of national elections is the attempt to measure attitudinal forces influencing Presidential vote choices developed by Donald Stokes.[3] His "component analysis" shown for four Presidential elections in Figure 5.4 takes into account the net impact of an attitudinal component on the vote and the strength of association between the attitudes and vote choice. The six attitudinal components represented by the bars as having a net pro-Democratic or pro-Republican impact in Figure 5.4 show the short-run forces causing deviations from basic partisan alignments in the electorate. This component analysis dramatizes the disastrous impact of the Goldwater candidacy in 1964. The bars also indicate the usual Republican advantage on foreign policy issues and a slight tendency for domestic issues to benefit Democratic candidates. The Democrats consistently benefit from the widespread perception that Democrats are

[3] Angus Campbell, *et al.*, *The American Voter*, pp. 524–31.

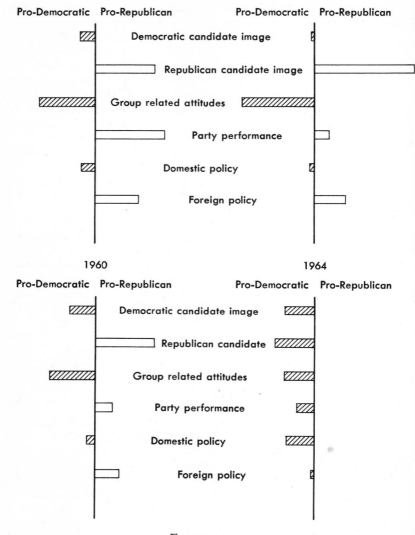

FIGURE 5.4
Attitudinal Component Analysis of the 1952, 1956, 1960 and 1964 Presidential Elections. (Survey Research Center, University of Michigan)

Source: These bar graphs were made from data provided in Donald Stokes, "Some Dynamic Elements of Contests for the Presidency," *American Political Science Review*, Vol. LX (March, 1966), pp. 19–28.

likely to help groups in the electorate with which voters identify. At the very least these attitudinal components represent the ideas and words which voters use to describe their feelings about the candidates.

During the conventions and the brief period of the campaign, political parties cannot do much about the basic partisan strength of each side so they concentrate on presenting candidate images and issue positions calculated to have greatest appeal to the uncommitted voters. Even if the outcome of an election is not substantially affected by party strategies, the content of the campaign and the meaning the election comes to have for leaders and the public are created by these strategies. Figure 5.4 can be viewed as measures of the content of the campaign and the meaning it has for the voters.

TYPES OF ELECTIONS

The late V. O. Key, a major political analyst of American elections, devised a set of categories for classifying elections, and while more elaborate versions of this scheme exist, these three categories will do for present purposes. The three types of elections are: "maintaining," "deviating" and "realigning" elections.

A maintaining election is one in which the stable, underlying partisan division in the electorate is directly reflected in the vote. The short-run forces associated with candidates and issues are not sufficient to change the outcome from what would be expected on the basis of normal party strength. By this definition the 1948 election of Truman, the 1960 election of Kennedy and the 1964 election of Johnson were maintaining elections with the basic Democratic advantage reflected in Democratic victories. The Eisenhower victories of 1952 and 1956 were deviating elections in which the short-run forces were strong enough to overcome the underlying partisan alignment; the candidates and issues caused a deviation from the outcome expected on the basis of normal party strength. According to the only analysis of expected vote for President compared with congressional voting over the full history of the United States,[4] the only candidates to inspire an extra "bonus vote" were popular military heroes although not all of these victories were deviating elections.

Realigning elections have been uncommon in American electoral history, and the period of 1928 and 1932 provided the most recent illustration. In realigning elections there is a substantial shift in the underlying partisan division and presumably such shifts accompany rather drastic social disruptions like those associated with severe depres-

[4] Charles Sellers, "The Equilibrium Cycle in Two-party Politics," *Public Opinion Quarterly*, Vol. XXIX (Spring, 1965), p. 22. The Presidents were Washington, Jackson, W. H. Harrison, Taylor, Grant, and Eisenhower.

sions and wars. Realigning elections or realigning periods account for the basic shifts in electoral patterns, but most political change is associated with more temporary deviating patterns.

The break in patterns of party voting in the 1890's is so closely associated with a major economic depression that the shift is quite similar to the early 1930's. As in 1930 the major break came in the congressional elections of 1894 two years before the presidential election in which McKinley defeated Bryan. This election has been interpreted as a conservative victory in the North but this should not be exaggerated. The Democratic Party in power was under Cleveland's conservative leadership, and rightly or wrongly the Democrats were held responsible for the depression just as the Republicans were after 1929. The congressional elections of 1894 broke patterns of political loyalty that had survived the Civil War in many areas. In one hundred years of electoral patterns the only dramatic shifts of basic partisan loyalty are directly related to major economic crises. While subsequent Presidential campaigns undoubtedly influenced these patterns, the major shifts did not appear to depend on the Presidential candidates of either 1896 or 1932. The main impetus appears to be a rejection of the party in power when the crisis occurs.

We cannot be certain that the shifts in basic partisan strength will be dramatic and result from social crises of some sort. It is also possible that shifts in party followings will occur gradually. The slow erosion of party followers over a decade could be just as important for the electoral system as more rapid change. The general assumption has been that only major social crises have the impact necessary to alter partisan loyalties, but the fundamental point is that the individual must be under such pressure that he changes his party identification. For this to happen to large numbers of people quickly a social crisis is probably necessary, but for this to happen to a large number of people over a decade or so independent events like individual social mobility might accomplish the same thing.

MEANING OF AN ELECTION

A persistent question in American politics is what election results mean. Politicians and news commentators spend much time and energy interpreting and explaining the outcome. It is easy to exaggerate the difficulties in assigning meaning to elections, but the most important element is usually quite clear—the winner. Elections are primarily a mechanism for selecting certain governmental leaders and, just as important, for removing leaders from office and preventing others from gaining office. Nevertheless an effort is often made to discover the policy implications of patterns of voting and read meaning into the outcome of elections. This effort raises two problems for analysis: first, the policy implications of winning and losing candidates' issue stands, and second, the issue content of the voters' decisions.

It is perfectly appropriate to attribute policy significance to an election on the basis of the policy preferences of the winning candidates so long as it is not implied that the voters had these policy implications in mind when they voted. That is, it is appropriate to observe that the election outcome means taxes will be lowered or a program expanded because the victor has pledged to lower taxes or expand the program. But it is very difficult to establish that the voters' preferences have certain policy meaning or that the votes for a particular candidate provide a policy mandate. There are several obstacles to stating simply what policies are implied by the voters' behavior. In many elections the voters are unaware of the candidates' stands on issues and sometimes the voters are mistaken in their perceptions of candidates' stands. Even if every voter knew that candidate A supported issue position X and that candidate B opposed X, that alone provides no basis for concluding that voters' preference for candidate A was based on his support of X.

Furthermore many voters are not concerned with issues in a campaign but vote according to their party loyalty. Presumably their vote has no particular policy significance but reflects a general preference for one party over another. If only those voters for whom the issues have some relevance to their decision are considered, statements can be made about the issues which helped a candidate win.

But at this point there is another difficulty. A crucial minority may swing to candidate C and give him a narrow victory because of his support of issue Y which is highly salient for this minority. It would be possible to say that candidate C won because of his support of issue Y, and yet it might also be true that the vast majority of voters who supported candidate C were opposed to issue Y but supported candidate C for other reasons. Is the election a mandate for or against policy Y? There is no correct answer to this question. What happens in the political system is that candidate C will try to select a course of action with respect to issue Y which will least jeopardize his chances for re-election. Candidate C has considerable freedom under these circumstances to interpret his victory with respect to issue Y. Most election outcomes are just this vague and conflicting with respect to most issues. This is a partial explanation of the failure of the American political system to impose policy stands on elected officials.

On the other hand generally there is no intense, widespread opposition to the stands of the candidate among his supporters. Voters will often vote for candidates who hold views not shared by the voters but these views are on matters of little interest to the voters. Presumably voters seldom support candidates who hold views with which they disagree intensely. In other words there is no intense, widespread opposition to the policies of the winning candidate but there may or may not be support for his policies. The main explanation of electoral support is still partisanship.

Campaigns and conventions, media coverage, party activities and general discussions provide the electorate with political information. For most the information is insufficient to motivate them to vote. For many voters, campaigns inspire some partisan enthusiasm and reinforce usual political commitments, and for others the campaign provides information which disturbs their customary vote patterns. The candidates and parties concentrate on arousing sympathetic responses in the electorate, but they must attempt this with an electorate whose opinions and loyalties are fairly set by the start of a campaign. For the most part they must work with situations they cannot greatly change. Campaign strategies aim at gaining an advantage in turnout among one's voters and at publicizing themes and symbols which arouse favorable sympathies. *The outcome of an election is mainly a result of the political preferences and patterns in the electorate and only slightly a result of the parties' strategy and maneuvering.* Since both parties in ordinary constituencies make substantial efforts during campaigns, their efforts may cancel one another. But neither party can afford to reduce its efforts. Furthermore even a relatively modest impact can change the outcome of close elections.

American elections are hardly a classic model of democracy with rational, well-informed voters making dispassionate decisions. On the other hand Americans provide an acceptable electoral opportunity for parties and candidates to attempt to win or hold public office. The electorate appears capable upon occasion to respond to issue appeals both positively and negatively but does not appear easily moved by most appeals. Traditional loyalties dominate electoral patterns and apparently reduce the possible instability of the electorate and its vulnerability to most appeals. In recent years the electorate has offered the parties modest opportunities to gain votes without offering extreme temptations to reckless appeals.

Survey Research Methods

So MANY OF THE DATA IN THIS BOOK HAVE COME FROM SURVEY research and so much of the analysis reported has been based on findings from survey research that some description of these methods may be necessary to establish their appropriateness. During the last thirty years social scientists have developed an impressive array of techniques for discovering and measuring individual attitudes and behavior. Basically survey research relies on giving a standard questionnaire to the individuals to be studied, and in most major studies of the national electorate trained interviewers ask the questions and record the responses in a face-to-face interview with each respondent. A few studies depend on the respondents to fill out the questionnaires themselves without using interviewers.

There are four data collection phases of survey research: 1) sampling, 2) interviewing, 3) questions, and 4) coding. At most points the methods of the Survey Research Center at the University of Michigan will be described.

SAMPLING

It may seem inappropriate to analyze the entire American electorate with studies composed of fewer than two thousand individuals, which is about the number of respondents in the studies used in this book. It would be prohibitively expensive to interview the entire electorate, and the only way to study public opinion nationally is by interviewing relatively few individuals who accurately represent the entire electorate. *Probability sampling is the method used to assure that the individuals selected for interviewing will be representative of the total population.*

Probability sampling attempts to select respondents in such a way that every individual in the population has an equal chance of being selected for interviewing. If the respondents are selected in this way, the analyst can be confident that the characteristics of the sample are approximately the same as those of the whole population. It would be impossibly difficult to make a list of every adult in the United States and then draw names from the list randomly so the Survey Research Center departs from such strict random procedures in three basic ways: the sample is *stratified, clustered,* and *of households.*

Stratification means that random selection occurs within sub-populations and in the United States customarily the sample is selected within regions to guarantee that all sections are represented and within communities of different sizes as well. Clustering means that within the geographical areas selected for sampling the interviews are concentrated in order to reduce the costs and inconvenience for interviewers. Finally, the Survey Research Center samples households rather than individuals (although within households individuals are sampled and interviewed) and this means that within sampling areas households are enumerated and selected at random. (This sampling procedure means that there are no interviews on military bases, in hospitals and prisons, or in other places where people do not live in households.)

An alternative procedure for selecting respondents is quota sampling and is employed commonly by commercial polling organizations. The areas where interviews are to be made may be picked by stratified sampling procedures but at the last stage of selection the interviewer is given discretion to choose respondents according to quotas. Quotas usually cover several social characteristics but the intention is to create a collection of respondents with proportions of quota-controlled characteristics identical to those in the population. For example, the quota might call for half the respondents to be men, half to be women; for one-third to be grade school educated, one-third high school educated and one-third college educated; and so forth. The advantage of this procedure is that it is much faster and less expensive than probability sampling, but the disadvantages are severe. With quota sampling the analyst cannot have confidence that respondents are representative of the total population because the interviewers introduce conscious or unconscious biases when selecting respondents. Both methods of sampling depend heavily on the ability and integrity of the interviewers, but probability sampling does not permit interviewers to introduce biases. Most statistical manipulations depend on using probability sampling.

INTERVIEWING

The selection of the sample depends on the interviewer but even more important is the role of the interviewer in asking questions of the respondent and recording the answers. Motivated, well-trained interviewers are crucial to the success of survey research. The interviewer has several major responsibilities: first, he selects the respondent according to sampling instructions; second, the interviewer must develop rapport with the respondent so he will be willing to go through with the interview which may last an hour or more; third, the interviewer must ask the questions in a friendly way and encourage the respondent to answer fully without distorting the answers; finally, the interviewer must record the answers of the respondent fully and accurately. In order to accomplish these tasks with a high level of proficiency the survey organizations train and retrain a permanent staff of interviewers.

QUESTIONS

Ordinarily in survey questionnaires several types of questions will be used. Public opinion surveys began years ago with forced choice questions to which a respondent was asked to give a simple answer. For example, forced choice questions frequently take the form of stating a position on public policy and asking the respondent to "agree" or "disagree" with the statement. The analysis in Chapter 4 was based on forced choice questions on public policy used in Survey Research Center questionnaires in which respondents were asked to "agree strongly," "agree," "disagree," or "disagree strongly." Some respondents give qualified answers that do not fit into these prearranged categories, or have no opinions.

The major innovation associated with the Survey Research Center is an alternative form of questioning called "open-ended." Open-ended questions give the respondent the opportunity to express his opinion in his own way without being forced to select among categories provided by the questionnaire. Questions like "Is there anything in particular you like about the Democratic Party?" or "What are the most important problems facing the country today?" permit the respondent to answer in his own terms. Survey Research Center interviewers encourage respondents to answer such questions as fully as they can with "probes" like "Could you tell me more about that," "anything else," and similar remarks that draw forth more discussion. There is no doubt that open-ended questions are a superior method of eliciting accurate expressions of opinion.

There are two major disadvantages in open-ended questioning:

one is that it places much more of a burden on interviewers to record the responses, and the other is that the burden of reducing the many responses to a dimension that can be analyzed is left for the coders. For example, in the United States if people are asked, "Do you think of yourself as a Democrat, a Republican or an independent?" almost all of the responses will fit usefully into the designated categories:

1. Democrat
2. Independent
3. Republican
4. Other party
5. I'm nothing, apolitical
6. Don't know
7. Refused to say
8. Not ascertained

On the other hand, if a relatively unstructured, open-ended question is used like "How do you think of yourself politically?" some people would answer with "Democrat," "Republican," etc. but many others would give answers that were quite different and not easily compared with the partisan categories. Often analysts intend to force responses into a single dimension like partisanship whether the respondents would have volunteered an answer along that dimension or not. This is essential if they are to develop single dimensions for analytic purposes. Modern survey research includes questions and techniques considerably more complex than these examples for establishing dimensions, but for the most part these methods have not been applied in political studies.

CODING

Once the interviewers administer the questionnaires to respondents, the coders take over and reduce the verbal information to a numerical form according to a "code." The numeric information unlike verbal information can be processed and manipulated by high speed data processing equipment. The coders' task may be simple or complex. For example, to code the respondent's sex requires a simple code:

1. Male
2. Female

This means that on an IBM card which contains information on the respondent a column will be designated for indicating the respondent's sex. A "1" punch in the column will indicate men and a "2" punch will indicate women. The code shown above for partisan categories gives the numbers that would stand for various responses.

Some coding is very complicated in that it requires elaborate arrays of categories and many columns on an IBM card. For example, coding of the responses to a question like "Is there anything in particular you don't like about the Democratic Party?" might include fifty or a hundred categories and these categories would cover such details as: "I like the party's farm policies," "I like the party's tax program," "I've just always been a Democrat." Some codes require the coders to make judgments about the respondents' answers and in political surveys these codes have covered judgments on the level of sophistication of the respondents' answers and judgments as to the main reason for respondents' vote choices. After the coders have converted the verbal information into numbers according to the coding instructions, the numbers are punched into IBM cards and readied for analysis. At this point the survey research process ends and the political analyst takes over to make what use of the data he can.

There are a number of good texts on survey research methods. The Survey Research Center has a *Manual For Interviewers* and a *Manual For Coders*;[1] these provide simple, thorough introductions to two phases of the data collection process. Leslie Kish's *Survey Sampling*[2] is by far the most authoritative and difficult work on sampling. Kahn and Cannel have provided a description and defense of the Survey Research Center interviewing in *The Dynamics of Interviewing*.[3] The best discussion of the use of survey research from the perspective of the social analyst is Herbert Hyman's *Survey Design and Analysis*.[4] The general introductions to social science methods include discussions of survey research, and the best are Festinger and Katz, *Research Methods in the Behavioral Sciences*[5] and Selltiz, *et al.*, *Research Methods in Social Relations*.[6] All major survey research organizations can provide descriptions of their methods, but the best single collection of questionnaires, codes and other methods from major political studies is available through the Inter-university Consortium for Political Research located at the University of Michigan.

[1] These manuals are available from the Survey Research Center at the University of Michigan.

[2] Leslie Kish, *Survey Sampling* (New York: John Wiley & Sons, Inc., 1965).

[3] Robert Kahn and Charles Cannel, *The Dynamics of Interviewing* (New York: John Wiley & Sons, Inc., 1957).

[4] Herbert Hyman, *Survey Design and Analysis* (Glencoe: The Free Press, 1955).

[5] Leon Festinger and Daniel Katz, eds., *Research Methods in the Behavioral Sciences* (New York: The Dryden Press, 1953).

[6] Claire Selltiz, *et al.*, *Research Methods in Social Relations* (New York: Holt, Rinehart and Winston, 1959).

Index

DATE DUE

FEB 24 '70	AUG 18 '76		
MAR 10 '70			
MAR 24 '70			
APR 7 '70			
MAY 12 '70			
FEB 12 '71			
FEB 25 '71			
MAR 1 '71			
JUL 28 '71			
AUG 17 '71			
DEC 15 '71			
FEB 16 '72			
JUN 26 '74			
AUG 5 '74			
JAN 31 '75			
FEB 14 '75			
FEB 28 '75			
AUG 10 '76			
GAYLORD			PRINTED IN U.S.A.